★ YOUR DAILY ★
PHIL

★ YOUR DAILY ★
PHIL

100 DAYS OF TRUTH AND FREEDOM TO HEAL AMERICA'S SOUL

PHIL ROBERTSON

NELSON
BOOKS

An Imprint of Thomas Nelson

CONTENTS

CONTENTS

PART III: HEALING

PART IV: FAITH

PART V: FAMILY

INTRODUCTION

Blessed is the nation whose God is the LORD,
the people he chose for his inheritance.
—PSALM 33:12

A merica was built on a godly foundation. Many (if not all) of the Founding Fathers considered the Bible as the framing of our country. They understood that virtue and morality couldn't exist without the influence of God. After all, these men had suffered greatly under the tyranny of a godless British king. So they came together to establish a republic firmly planted on the principles of God's Word, knowing that as long as we stayed true to our biblical foundation, America would be as enduring as the Scriptures themselves.

But what did we do? Our politicians booted God out of schools, tried to boot God out of their platforms, and started promoting the slaughter of children in the womb. They removed the statues, signs, and symbols of our country's biblical heritage from the public square. They knelt for chaos and stood for evil.

With God and his Word effectively canceled out of our culture, the idea began to spread that all truth is relative. The prevailing attitude of the day is: *Follow your own desires and make your own truth.* In today's America, everyone's personal truth must be accepted and celebrated—that is, except for biblical morality. That is the one truth that must be silenced at all costs.

It's clear that the enemy of our country's soul has come to steal, kill, and destroy everything our Founding Fathers stood for. How has he shattered America's soul? He's done it through division, hatred, and the dismantling of our nation's biblical foundation.

What can help bridge these divisions and heal our nation? Can secular humanists, smooth-talking celebrities, or progressive politicians unify us? They haven't yet—and they never will. Spiritual problems need spiritual solutions, not political ones.

The truth is, governments and ideologies can't remove sin, and they can't defeat death. They just can't do it. There will never be hope in hollow and deceptive philosophies full of "your truth" and "his truth" and "her truth." There is only one truth, and we need a mass awakening to it:

> Jesus answered, "I am the way and the truth and the life. No one comes to the Father except through me." (John 14:6)

There's a simple solution to all our disunity, and it's the absolute truth of God's Word. We can return to the Almighty and understand how he has created us to be unified under his message that we all are created in his image, and he loves us all without distinction.

Jesus came to destroy the divisions between people, to bring all of us into the family of everlasting life. After his death, burial, resurrection, and ascension, he sent the Spirit of the Almighty to the disciples; and through that Spirit he showed them just how he intends to bring people of all makes and models into the fold.

Well, listen up: America won't make it another generation without the healing that comes from Christians who are committed to living out the truth of God's Word. Our nation needs Christians who will live out our faith by doing what we can do *every day* to love God, love our neighbor, and do what's right—no matter who's running the government. That's the only way the soul of our nation will be healed.

In this 100-day reader we will focus on the God-honoring principles that will heal America's soul. If you're serious about being the kind of Christian who can make a real difference in our nation, then join me as we discover how to stand firm in our faith and lead our families well by championing the truth and freedom that come only from God and his Word.

★ PART I ★
TRUTH

LOVE DOES NOT DELIGHT IN EVIL BUT
REJOICES WITH THE TRUTH.

—1 CORINTHIANS 13:6

DAY 1 ★ IS GOD DEAD?

The LORD is the true God;
  he is the living God, the eternal King.
—JEREMIAH 10:10

In April 1966 *Time* raised a ruckus when it printed this question on its cover: "Is God Dead?"

It was a shocking cover posing a shocking question, and that question took root in the public dialogue of the day. Scientists, preachers, insurance agents, housewives—everyone from New York to California was drawn into the discussion. Even us river rats down in Northern Louisiana. But if the cover was provocative, the story inside the magazine was even more provocative.

"Is God dead?" the article asked. "A small band of radical theologians has seriously argued that the churches must accept the fact of God's death, and get along without him."[1]

Huh?

The disappearance of God in art, politics, and economics led to the death of God, some claimed in the article. Modern science had undermined or explained the mysteries of God in the natural world, others said.

This *Time* article explored the very things I'd hear on my college campus at Louisiana Tech University later that year. Man's ancestors crawled out of the salt water, they said. Man's notions of right and wrong were taught, handed down; morality was a set of fabricated human constructs, they said. Morality was relative. Sexuality was relative. Nothing was absolute. God, the old white-bearded judge in the sky, was a myth. What's more, professor after professor implied that if man could liberate himself from this archaic myth, he'd find true freedom.

Man could be his own judge.

Man could be his own master.

Man could be the arbiter of his own freedom.

Man could be the center of his own existence.

It's been more than fifty years since the publication of that *Time* article, and almost as many years since I was freed from the lies written about in that article. How was I freed? Only through an encounter with the living God.

The last time I checked, God ain't dead. He is very much alive. It's a fact. What's more, the polls I've seen indicate that the vast majority of Americans know this to be true. Nearly 90 percent of Americans believe in God.[2] But despite the fact that God isn't dead, despite the fact that the majority of us believe that to be true, why do so many Americans seem to continue toward death and destruction?

I suppose the Devil makes them do it.

Time presented Friedrich Nietzsche's thesis: "Self-centered man had killed God, and that settled that." Here's what Nietzsche failed to realize: that declaration was far from settled. Here's what else he failed to realize: if the God of the Bible is dead, man has no hope of experiencing eternal life. Of course, Nietzsche discovered that truth just after he took his last breath. Nanoseconds after crossing over death's threshold, the German philosopher stood at the judgment seat of the wild, fearsome Lord of the universe, the living God.

It's been four decades since my encounter with God, and I can tell you, I'm not running from anyone or anything; I'm not enslaved to the -isms of the world. And if America would awaken to that same truth, the truth and good news Jesus came to bring us, it might just change everything.

★   ★   ★

Lord, I praise you for being the living God, who reigns forever. In a nation deceived by the lies of the Devil, help me to focus on the truth, knowing that you are very much alive and at work in the world today.

DAY 2 ★ THE LIES OF THE DECEIVER

He was a murderer from the beginning, not
holding to the truth, for there is no truth in him.
When he lies, he speaks his native language,
for he is a liar and the father of lies.
—JOHN 8:44

Despite our nation's biblical foundation, America's most influential thinkers and leaders began to say, "God is dead," trying to convince themselves it was true. And as they said it over and over again, they began to tell themselves this too: *truth is dead, or at least relative.*

Questioning the absolute truth of God's existence opens the door to all sorts of other questions too.

- If God is dead, what does he have to say? *Nothing.*
- If his word isn't true, what is the Bible but a good story and an ancient moral code? *Probably nothing.*
- If the Bible is nothing more than a good story, is there really an evil one himself? *It's doubtful.*
- If the Bible is only an ancient moral code, how can it apply today? *It probably doesn't.*
- If it doesn't apply, can there be a penalty for breaking that moral standard? Can there be a hell? *It's uncertain at best.*
- If there's no hell, why did Christ die? *Who knows, really? He was probably just a lunatic.*

This is the way it all breaks down, see. If the very existence of God is in question, then so are the absolute truths spoken by that God in the Bible. At best those truths are relative, they argue, and if all truth is relative, then aren't we free to chase our desires? What's keeping us from acting on every sexual impulse? Why not say what we want, drink what we want, take every advantage we can get? Why not abort babies, steal, murder? If there's no absolute standard for truth, who can say these things are wrong?

As I see it, there's only one problem with this line of thinking, and it's a big problem. It's all based on the lie that God is dead. A lie created by the deceiver himself, Satan.

Throughout the Bible the evil one has been known as a deceiver, a liar, and the lawless one. Jesus said he was a murderer and a liar from the beginning. As he said in the gospel of John, "When he lies, he speaks his native language, for he is a liar and the father of lies" (8:44). Paul told us that he comes disguised as an angel of light (2 Cor. 11:14). Maybe like one of those enlightened university professors, modern scientists, or politicians.

Though Satan has deceived men over and over again, Paul warned us of his schemes. He taught us exactly how the Devil and his end-time servant, the lawless one, operate. In his second letter to the Thessalonians, Paul wrote,

> The coming of the lawless one will be in accordance with how Satan works. He will use all sorts of displays of power through signs and wonders that serve the lie, and all the ways that wickedness deceives those who are perishing. They perish because they refused to love the truth and so be saved. For this reason God sends them a powerful delusion so that they will believe the lie and so that all will be condemned who have not believed the truth but have delighted in wickedness. (2:9–12)

Lies, lies, lies—they're the only weapon the evil one has in his arsenal. He uses those weapons against the human race, trying to deceive them so they'll turn away from God. So they'll forget his truths and chase their own desires down to death.

See? When God is dead, so is his divine truth. And without divine truth, without truth to govern our human conduct, we fall for the Devil's lie.

★   ★   ★

God, so many people in our nation have been blinded by the lies of the Devil. We need your truth, revealed in your Word! Help me to study the Scriptures and share your truth with others.

DAY 3 ★ THE TRUTH THAT SETS US FREE

Then you will know the truth, and the truth will set you free.
—JOHN 8:32

We live in a dark day, a day when the Devil has indwelled so many and whispered, *All truth is relative*. He's convinced us there's no absolute moral standard for sexuality (which the Bible confines to the marital bed). There's no absolute truth regarding when life begins (which the Bible says begins before the first cells are knit in the womb). There's no absolute truth about the definition of marriage (which the Bible indicates as being between one man and one woman, till death do they part). There's no timeless and absolute truth about virtue or law or even what constitutes the church.

Everything is up in the air, the liar says, *so follow your own desires and make your own truth*.

Can there be any doubt that America has fallen under the delusion of the evil one? And yes, this is bad news. But here's the good news, the gospel news: Jesus came to show us the truth that would set us free from the evil one's delusions (John 8:32). Again, look at the writings of Paul:

> Like the rest, we were by nature deserving of wrath. But because of his great love for us, God, who is rich in mercy, made us alive with Christ even when we were dead in transgressions—it is by grace you have been saved. And God raised us up with Christ and seated us with him in the heavenly realms in Christ Jesus, in order that in the coming ages he might show the incomparable riches of his grace, expressed in his kindness to us in Christ Jesus. (Eph. 2:3–7)

God saved us from evil. He saved us from wrath. He saved us because of his great love for us, and for what purpose? So that he could show us "the incomparable riches of his grace."

Sounds like a good deal if you ask me.

And once we're freed from sin and wrath, how do we live into those incomparable riches? We stake our lives on the absolute truth of the Bible.

What does the Bible say about the truth?

I'm glad you asked.

The Bible is God's written Word, and it contains his eternal, divine, and timeless truth. Repeatedly, King David, the man after God's own heart, recognized the truth of God's Word. In Psalm 25:5 (NKJV) he wrote, "Lead me in Your truth and teach me, for you are the God of my salvation." Likewise, in Psalm 33:4 he wrote, "For the word of the LORD is right and true; he is faithful in all he does." Psalm 119:142, a psalm often attributed to David, reads, "Your righteousness is everlasting and your law is true." Over and over, the Bible reminds us: God's Word is the absolute, unchanging truth that sets us free.

God, thank you for your Word, the absolute, unshakable truth that abides forever. I pray that our nation—including my family and me— will experience healing by embracing the truth that sets us free.

DAY 4 ★ THE BLESSINGS OF TRUTH

I am the way and the truth and the life. No one comes to the Father except through me.
—JOHN 14:6

Christ himself said there is objective and absolute truth. In fact, he went a step further. He claimed *he* was the absolute truth, saying, "I am the way and the truth and the life. No one comes to the Father except through me" (John 14:6). What was Jesus' message? There was no way to break free from the delusions of the enemy but to trust in his message and walk in his ways.

In his letter to the Ephesians, Paul wrote that the Gentiles believed the lies of the Devil and engaged in "every kind of impurity, and they [were] full of greed" (4:19). However, the Ephesian church had been taught a different way, the way of righteousness and holiness. Paul wrote,

> That, however, is not the way of life you learned when you heard about Christ and were taught in him in accordance with *the truth that is in Jesus.* You were taught, with regard to your former way of life, to put off your old self, which is being corrupted by its deceitful desires; to be made new in the attitude of your minds; and to put on the new self, created to be like God in true righteousness and holiness. (vv. 20–24, emphasis added)

The Bible promises that if we live according to his absolute truth and try our best to live sinless, godly lives, we'll enjoy the blessings of God. It also promises this: if we follow the truth, we'll be weird folks. John wrote it this way: "The reason the world does not know us is that it did not know him" (1 John 3:1). But if we remain faithful, we'll not only gain peace of mind and eternal life, we'll have the opportunity to influence some of our opponents. Why else would Paul instruct,

10

Opponents must be gently instructed, in the hope that God will grant them repentance leading them to a knowledge of the truth, and that they will come to their senses and escape from the trap of the devil, who has taken them captive to do his will. (2 Tim. 2:25–26)

Even those who've been indwelled by the evil one can be freed. I was.

We're two thousand years away from the incarnation of Christ, who had lived a morally perfect life of love, died as a sacrifice for our sins, and beat the grave so we, too, might beat it one day. We're two thousand years away from the writings of the apostles, the early followers of Christ who taught us to live like Christ, with lives of righteous, holy love. We're two thousand years away, but here's the thing about absolute truth: it doesn't change with time. It's as solid as petrified cypress. As immovable too.

So the world can claim that God has died and his truth has passed away with him. They can say all truth is relative, that it can be changed with the shifting desires of men. They can say I'm a crazy, uneducated, Bible-thumping river rat. They can say and say and say. You know what my response will be?

The truth ain't a buzzkill, dude. It'll give you life, peace of mind, and make you happy, happy, happy.

Lord, help me to be courageous and boldly live out my faith, no matter what others may say. Thank you for your promise that those who live according to your absolute truth will be happy, happy, happy, both in this world and in the world to come.

DAY 5 ★ STUDYING THE TRUTH

Sanctify them by the truth; your word is truth.
—JOHN 17:17

The power of God—who knew it could change a river rat's heart? As a new Christian, I gave myself to this power the best way I knew how. I committed to reading the Bible every day. I treated it as if it were bread and water, and the only way I could eat and drink it was through my eyes and ears.

I was utterly desperate for the Scriptures. In the mornings I read before the boys awoke. Between classes I'd pull a copy from my desk drawer and wade into it. After one of Miss Kay's famous home-cooked meals, after the boys were bathed, after they'd settled in for the night, I'd settle into reading the Word. I read it so much, I inadvertently began committing certain passages to memory. It turns out, the Bible was the truth, and the truth was setting me free.

When I wasn't immersed in the Scriptures, I was immersed in the things of God at church. I continued to attend the Bible study with those reformed bandits, the river rats and rednecks who'd accepted Christ just like I had. But as I grew into my faith, as I rooted into church like a backwater cypress, I met other men, men of repute like Tommy Powell, Doyle Jennings, Bill Johnson, Lynn Campbell, and J. J. Turner, who wanted nothing more than to advance God's agenda on the earth. Their commitment to living upright lives in accordance with the truth of God's Word had led to success, and I figured I could learn something from them. So I attended their Bible classes and hung on their every word. They became my big brothers in the faith, and they showed me how their commitment to the absolute truth of the Scriptures had led to their success. This is not to say they were all wealthy, of course, but they had everything they needed. More than that, they were free.

As I surveyed the good churchmen around me, I noted how they'd been blessed. Best as I could tell, they'd been found trustworthy enough to be blessed by God, and they shared those blessings with the community. Trustworthiness—*what a deal.*

Before God had wrestled me out of the muddy banks of the Ouachita, I was the most untrustworthy redneck. I was all about the party, all about whoring around. I was all about poaching ducks and running the back roads drunk. Restraint was boredom. Law-abiding was its own prison cell. I lied when I had to. Cheated too. My desire drove me, and I made my own rules, set my own boundaries. The truth was relative, at least as far as I was concerned. But that was before the truth of Jesus came calling, before it showed me that my lack of restraint was the real prison, a prison of death. And now that I'd come to believe in Jesus, I wanted to be found faithful, trustworthy.

God, thank you for your Word, which is truth. Stir up in me a desire to study the Scriptures, and teach me your truth so that I may be found faithful and trustworthy.

DAY 6 ★ THE TRUTH THAT PROVIDES

**Look at the birds of the air; they do not sow
or reap or store away in barns, and yet
your heavenly Father feeds them.**
—MATTHEW 6:26

By the summer of 1977, I was building my duck call business and fishing to make ends meet. In the early mornings I'd run the trotlines, hoop nets, and trammel nets up and down the Ouachita River. The banks of that river had once provided for Native Americans. It'd provided for the local rednecks. Now it was providing for me and my family.

Morning after morning, setting those lines, I took comfort in the ways God provided for his creatures. The deer had acorns from the forest on either side of the river. Where the bottoms flattened out, a steady supply of wild millet, wild sunflowers, and sprangletop cropped up to feed the migrating ducks. The coyotes, beavers, foxes, and feral cats had everything they needed. What's more, the river rats, rednecks, and trappers—folks just like me—had all we needed to make ends meet. With new eyes to see the goodness of God, the words of Jesus came to mind: "Look at the birds of the air; they do not sow or reap or store away in barns, and yet your heavenly Father feeds them" (Matt. 6:26).

Those were the poorest years of my life, and some of my most labor intensive too. I fished, hunted, and trapped while the sun was up, and worked on my prototype duck calls in the meantime. But poor as we were, the absolute truth of God's Word stood. Not only had he rescued me from sin, shame, and certain death, but he was providing more than enough for my family's needs. In fact, on any given night, Miss Kay and I would host church folks of all shapes, sizes, and colors. They'd come with a pan of crackling bread or a pot of beans. We'd fry catfish from the river. We'd give thanks, break bread, and sing praises to the Lord for his goodness. Together we learned what it meant to share all things in common, just like the first church did (Acts 2:44). Together we learned what the truth of the Scriptures meant—God really did provide for his faithful people.

I created my first duck call, whittled from scrap wood lying around my home. I tested it on the river and discovered what I already believed to be true: I could command ducks with that call. Trouble was, without machinery, I couldn't produce the calls to scale. The other trouble was, without money, I couldn't procure machinery.

My fellow church member Baxter Brasher said my prototype was the best call he'd ever heard and helped me procure a $25,000 loan to purchase the lathe I needed to ramp up production. Baxter agreed to help me because he'd seen how committed I'd been to the Word of Truth. He'd seen how I'd trusted the Lord's providence and took a leap of faith. He watched as Miss Kay and I shared all we had with whoever needed it. He said he'd found me to be a faithful student of our Master, and he knew if I continued to live my life in the absolute truth of God's Word, if I continued to dedicate myself to the craft God had blessed me with, I'd do just fine.

Baxter was right. I reckon I've done just fine. I haven't missed a meal yet.

★   ★   ★

Lord, thank you for your Word, which assures us that you provide for your creation. Help me to trust your providence as I commit to living out your Word of Truth.

DAY 7 ★ THE POWERFUL, UNCHANGING TRUTH

The grass withers and the flowers fall,
but the word of our God endures forever.
—ISAIAH 40:8

The truth of God's Word is solid, unchanging, and sure. My life is a testament to it. I'd believed the truth of the Scriptures and went all in. The Bible said I could be freed from sin and shame, and it was true. The Bible said a moral and godly life would bring peace of mind, and it did. The Scriptures also said the Lord would bless and provide for his children who walk in the truth, and time after time, he did that too. Now, after years of believing and following this truth, I've seen firsthand the difference Christ can make in a life, a business, a television show, and ultimately, across a nation.

The way I see it, either I am the luckiest redneck in all of Northern Louisiana, or God blesses those who make an unwavering commitment to follow God's Word. And seeing as how my life was anything but lucky until I followed the truth, I reckon I know the truth.

As believers in Jesus, as members of the church, we have access to the ultimate truth: God is alive and active, and he wants to save us from the hell of our own anger, hatred, and sin. He wants to save us from actual hell too. It's the most powerful truth there is, the truth that might save the soul of America from the devastating consequences of sin.

If this truth is so powerful, why doesn't it seem to be taking hold? Why does it seem that the powerful message of the gospel is absent in the world around us?

As much as it pains me to say it, I think the answer is plain. The church has forgotten its purpose, forgotten that we're supposed to be carrying the truth of the Almighty out to the world. Instead, we've hidden our message under a bushel. We've kept our message locked up in a two-hour Sunday morning service and gone along with the rest of the world during the other 166 hours of the week.

The people of God—the very mouthpieces of Christ himself—have forgotten the essence of true worship. Is it any wonder we've lost so much ground in America?

America, this is where the rubber meets the road. You either believe in the absolute truth of the Bible, or you don't. You either repent and return to God's standard of living, or you continue to believe the lies of Satan and reap the heartache of evil. As for me and my house? We'll follow the truth, thank you very much, and if I had my way, America would test the promises of God and see that they are given to us in love. Americans would find the peace of mind, unity, and prosperity they so want.

Lord, as for me and my house, we will follow you. Give me courage and boldness as I carry your powerful, unchanging, absolute truth out to the world.

DAY 8 ★ THE AUTHOR AND SUSTAINER OF TRUE LIFE

Through him all things were made; without him nothing was made that has been made.
—JOHN 1:3

In my college years, I ran up on some enlightened professors who taught us that we'd evolved from apes some millions of years ago. Where did the apes come from? Good question, they said. The apes evolved from fish, which had grown legs and crawled from the salt water onto the land. Where'd the fish come from? They'd evolved from single cells, had doubled up and grown tails. Where'd the single cells come from? They'd been swimming around in the salt water since just after the big bang, the professors said.

Huh?

I didn't ever believe the lie that men had evolved from apes, or fish, or single cells that crawled out of the salt water. I was a man of the woods, and I'd never seen a catfish crawl out of the mud and turn into an ape. And sure, I hadn't been around for millions of years, but common sense is common sense. Nope, I didn't really believe in evolution at all. But until I came to know the power of Jesus in my life, I didn't stop to consider the simplest question: Where had all this life come from?

After running up on Jesus, I'd found the peace of mind I so wanted. And as I came to understand the absolute truth of his Word, as I ate the Scriptures day after day, I found that the Almighty really was the source of the fullest life. In Genesis I read how God created the heavens and earth, how he started with light, then created fish, plants, and animals before making man. I read the gospel of John and through it discovered that the creative process had occurred through

Jesus himself. "Through him all things were made; without him nothing was made that has been made," John wrote (John 1:3). I read the words of Paul to the Colossians, too, read how "in him all things were created: things in heaven and on earth, visible and invisible, whether thrones or powers or rulers or authorities; all things have been created through him and for him" (1:16).

Not only had Christ been the creating agent of all life; he'd also come to bring life where the enemy of our souls had tried to bring death. Jesus put it plainly in the book of John: "The thief comes only to steal and kill and destroy; I have come that they may have life, and have it to the full" (10:10). He didn't just say it, though. As the Author and Sustainer of all life, he backed up his words as he walked among the people. He raised a dead man, Lazarus, to new life (John 11:38–44). He raised Jairus's daughter from death to life (Mark 5:21–43). He even took five loaves of bread and two fish and multiplied it to feed more than five thousand people (Matt. 14:13–21). That act of creating food for so many hungry people—bread and fish—wasn't that a life-giving act? And this is nothing to say of the fact that Jesus came to free us from eternal death and raise us to everlasting life.

The Scriptures couldn't be clearer. The Almighty is the Author and Sustainer of true life, and he works his purposes out through Jesus Christ.

★   ★   ★

God, I praise you for being the Author and Sustainer of all life. Thank you for sending your Son, Jesus, to set me free from eternal death and raise me to everlasting life.

DAY 9 ★ RETURN TO THE TRUTH

God . . . gives life to everything.
—1 TIMOTHY 6:13

Death, chaos, and mass murder. It's a slaughterhouse out there, a real meat grinder, and is it any wonder? If we've killed God, why not kill a man or two? If we've killed God, what are the consequences for our acts of murder?

And they call me crazy for killing ducks?

The liberal politicians, university professors, and talking heads on the news offer different reasons for the uptick in these kinds of mass murders. They point to study after study and pin the blame on the gun industry. They talk about mental health issues. And though they are well meaning, these folks fail to recognize the true root of the problem: men do not respect the image of God in their fellow man. Why? They don't believe God created man in the first place. Having taken God out of the equation, having failed to retain the knowledge of God, the wicked men of America have been given over to their depraved minds. They've become just like their father, the evil one—a liar and murderer from the beginning.

I've retained the truth of God's Word and know that he has authored all life for my benefit and sustenance. I know all life the Almighty created—plants, animals, and my fellow man—points me always to God's invisible qualities, his care, love, and protection. And by reading the Scriptures, I know that Jesus Christ is the ultimate embodiment of that life, that he came to show us how to live it to the full. He came to free us from eternal death and bring us to eternal life too. It's that truth that anchors my soul and brings me great peace.

Life—see? It's a gift from God.

From time to time good folks ask me how we might decrease abortion or gang violence or mass shootings. They ask if we should change abortion laws or whether we should create stricter gun legislation. They ask whether government policies can make a difference. I tell them I don't know, but I doubt it. I don't reckon any amount of legislation can change the hearts of those under the influence of the evil one. There is an antidote, though, and it's simple.

America, return to the truth.

How?

Remember God, the Author of life, and see how he's created all life to nourish and sustain us. As you remember, partner with the Almighty in tending to life. Leave the slaughterhouse and get out to nature. Cultivate and harvest a little. See how tender the life he's created is, how tasty it is too. And as you see the beauty of God in his nature, recognize the beauty in the life of your fellow man also. See how he was created in the image of God. Remember that his blood ain't yours to take, whether the blood of an unborn baby or an elderly woman minding her business in a Texas church. Return to the truth. Choose life. And when you do, watch as God saves your soul. And then give thanks.

★　　★　　★

God, help me to remember that you are the Author of life and will nourish and sustain us. May our nation return to your truth and choose life, which is a gift from you.

DAY 10 ★ THE NARROW ROAD
OF GOD'S TRUTH

**Enter through the narrow gate. For wide is the gate
and broad is the road that leads to destruction, and
many enter through it. But small is the gate and narrow
the road that leads to life, and only a few find it.**
—MATTHEW 7:13-14

My morning routine is regular. Unwavering. Predictable. After I wake up and throw on my camo, I have a few cups of sturdy coffee. Then I leave the house, and when I get to the end of my driveway, I'm faced with a decision. Should I take a left and make my way to town, or should I take a right and head down the narrower road that leads to the woods? The road to town is wider and better paved. It leads to places like the grocery store, church, or Miss Kay's Eats & Sweets—all fine and good places. But those roads also lead away from the quieter fields of God. Many of those roads lead to the virtueless places of American society. So, nine times out of ten, I take the narrow road to the woods.

In duck season the narrow roads lead me to my flooded fields and the blinds, and there I set out the decoys and prepare for a harvest. In the off-season, though, the season when the fields aren't flooded, I ride around the fields in my Yamaha and tend to my plot. I take out undesirable weeds that choke out the good grasses and cut down the trees that will eventually block my shooting lanes. As I work in the quietness of the great outdoors, there's a fragrant peace.

As narrow as the road is that leads me into the woods—only wide enough for my Yamaha—there are narrow paths that wild game use to get from field to stream. These narrow trails lead to feeding grounds or places where the deer bed down. They lead to watering holes or the beavers' den. These are some of my favorite places in the woods because they support so much innocent life. I can spend hours just watching these trails, and as I do, guess what? I live a sin-free life.

Alone in the woods, it's possible to go a whole day without sinning, nutty as that may sound. Walking alone in the fields and praying, watching the game running up and down the pig trails, it's unlikely you'll use the Lord's name in vain or worship some other god. In the woods there's no one to steal from, no women to lust after. There's no one to lie to either, and you can't murder someone who's not around. Sin management in isolation is easy, see.

I suspect our Founding Fathers knew most people wouldn't participate in sin management by making their way to the woods. They knew that our great America wouldn't be forged in isolation, and that most people would congregate down the wider roads. They knew folks would rub shoulders as they built the great society. And they hoped these folks—together with all their children and grandchildren— would build a strong and virtuous nation. They knew, though, that any community of people hoping to build a virtuous society would need a teacher. And so they left us the ultimate instructor: a canon of biblically based law.

God, thank you for giving us your law, which reveals to us your truth. May I build upon our nation's strong and virtuous foundation by choosing the narrow road that leads to life.

DAY 11 ★ THE ETERNAL KINGDOM

The God of heaven will set up a kingdom that will never be destroyed, nor will it be left to another people. It will crush all those kingdoms and bring them to an end, but it will itself endure forever.
—DANIEL 2:44

America was founded on the rule of law. Our Founding Fathers created a system of laws based on God's Word. It was a system framed by the Constitution, and it was meant to protect religious liberty, promote personal responsibility, support American families, protect the innocent, value integrity and morality, and guard against the tyranny of monarchies. It was a legal system with checks and balances, one in which the United States Supreme Court was meant to ensure that every law in this country lined up with the Constitution framed by our Founders.

America's legal system started out on the right foot. Based in God's Word, with a legislature that began the day with prayer and subject to a court whose building had a depiction of Moses and the Ten Commandments on it, we were on the right track. And though we didn't get it perfect, we were still pointed in a God-honoring direction. But Americans are no different than other humans, and we've lost sight of our godly heritage. Like every other people who've ever existed, we're prone to wander.

Lord, I feel it.

I've seen that wandering over my life, a wandering that gets worse as the years roll by. And if we'd wake up long enough to notice, we'd find we're wandering toward the edge of a high cliff. And if world history is any indication, I suspect we'll eventually wander over the edge of that cliff just as other countries have, even to our ruin. After all, there's only one kingdom that stands forever, and it's certainly not America.

Earthly kingdoms come and go. The Scriptures say as much. In fact, the Almighty spoke to King Nebuchadnezzar in a dream. Unable to interpret the dream, the king called Daniel, a young Jewish man, and asked for the meaning. Unashamed and unafraid, Daniel recounted the dream:

> There before you stood a large statue—an enormous, dazzling statue, awesome in appearance. The head of the statue was made of pure gold, its chest and arms of silver, its belly and thighs of bronze, its legs of iron, its feet partly of iron and partly of baked clay. . . . A rock was cut out, but not by human hands. It struck the statue on its feet of iron and clay and smashed them. (Dan. 2:31–34)

Daniel explained that Babylon, represented by the golden head, would give way to an inferior silver kingdom (the Persian Empire). The silver kingdom would fall to the bronze kingdom (the Greek Empire). That bronze kingdom would give way to an iron kingdom, which would become divided (the divided Roman Empire in the days of Jesus). And in those days, the eternal kingdom would come. Daniel said:

> In the time of those kings, the God of heaven will set up a kingdom that will never be destroyed, nor will it be left to another people. It will crush all those kingdoms and bring them to an end, but it will itself endure forever. (v. 44)

The empires of the earth, with their man-made government structures and legal codes, would be crushed by the rock, the eternal kingdom. As Jesus said, "On this rock, I will build my church, and the gates [or the kingdom] of Hades will not overcome it" (Matt. 16:18).

God, you are the only King whose kingdom will endure forever. Help me to build my life on the enduring foundation of your Word.

DAY 12 ★ TEN SIMPLE LAWS

**The law was our guardian until Christ came
that we might be justified by faith.**
—GALATIANS 3:24

God created us to live in relationship with him and each other. He created us in love for love. But even from the beginning, men had trouble living with one another, much less loving one another. Eve tricked Adam. Cain killed Abel. A whole world of folks in Noah's day and age were violent and unruly. Without some code, some law or governing authority of men, they were bent on evil.

After the Almighty freed his people from Egypt, he knew they'd need some code, some set of laws if they were going to make it. So, in his graciousness, the one Lawgiver and Judge himself gave his people an exact, objective standard to govern their conduct. He gave them a tool to instruct them on how to build a godly and loving society. What was that tool? The law.

In the Exodus account, we find God's people wandering in the desert. Freed from the tyrannical rule of Egypt's pharaoh, they were forming a new nation. Knowing this nation would need a code of conduct, rules for leading them into understanding their relationship to God and one another, God called Moses to Mount Sinai, and he gave them ten simple laws written on stone tablets (20:3–17). What were those ten laws?

1. You shall have no other gods before me.
2. You shall not make for yourself an image in the form of anything in heaven above or on the earth beneath or in the waters below. You shall not bow down to them or worship them.
3. You shall not misuse the name of the Lord your God,

for the LORD will not hold anyone guiltless who misuses his name.

4. Remember the Sabbath day by keeping it holy. Six days you shall labor and do all your work, but the seventh day is a Sabbath to the LORD your God.

5. Honor your father and your mother, so that you may live long in the land the LORD your God is giving you.

6. You shall not murder.

7. You shall not commit adultery.

8. You shall not steal.

9. You shall not give false testimony against your neighbor.

10. You shall not covet your neighbor's house. You shall not covet your neighbor's wife, or his male or female servant, his ox or donkey, or anything that belongs to your neighbor.

The law was given to the people of Israel to teach them how to love both God and their neighbors. It was the basis of their well-ordered society. Truth is, those Ten Commandments probably didn't contain any real surprises—honor God alone; don't kill; don't steal; don't lie; respect your parents; don't cheat on your wife. Common sense should tell you these things will help a society run more smoothly. Still, God gave them the written law as a reminder for when the people of Israel were tempted to stray. The law served as their guide, or as Paul wrote in his letter to the Galatians, it was their "guardian until Christ came" (3:24).

★　　★　　★

God, thank you for giving the law as a tool for building a godly and loving society. As a Christian living under grace, help me to respect your Ten Commandments as an enduring basis of a well-ordered nation.

DAY 13 ★ THE PERFECT SOURCE OF LAW

This command is a lamp,
  this teaching is a light,
and correction and instruction
  are the way to life.
—PROVERBS 6:23

Over and over, the people of Israel were urged to listen to the law of Moses as passed down from their mothers and fathers. Solomon wrote,

> My son, keep your father's command
>   and do not forsake your mother's teaching.
> Bind them always on your heart;
>   fasten them around your neck. (vv. 20–21)

Solomon promised that if the people obeyed God's instructions, the law would watch over them when they slept, speak to them when they awoke, guide them like a lamp, and show them the way to life (vv. 22–23). When followed, the law would bring peace with God and their neighbors.

But what about those who weren't Israelites? How could they order their lives since they didn't have the law? Paul recognized there are certain absolute truths all people know. There is something in all people that shows them right from wrong. He wrote,

> Indeed, when Gentiles, who do not have the law, do by nature things required by the law, they are a law for themselves, even though they do not have the law. They show that the requirements

of the law are written on their hearts, their consciences also bearing witness, and their thoughts sometimes accusing them and at other times even defending them. (Rom. 2:14–15)

And just as the law of the Israelites was meant to guide the people in learning to love God and each other, the law written on people's hearts could be summed up in one word: *love*. Paul wrote,

Let no debt remain outstanding, except the continuing debt to love one another, for whoever loves others has fulfilled the law. The commandments, "You shall not commit adultery," "You shall not murder," "You shall not steal," "You shall not covet," and whatever other command there may be, are summed up in this one command: "Love your neighbor as yourself." Love does no harm to a neighbor. Therefore love is the fulfillment of the law. (Rom. 13:8–10)

In other words, if people simply acted in love toward others, they wouldn't violate any of the Ten Commandments. They wouldn't lie, cheat, or steal.

See how powerful love is?

Our Founding Fathers understood the value of the law of Moses. They knew that any group of people living together would have difficulty living the perfect law of love, so they framed our republic with the timbers of biblical truth, biblical law. They knew that only by living godly lives—lives ordered by God's laws—would we ever achieve lasting peace and prosperity.

Over and over, the leaders of our country have recognized the importance of the Bible in framing our legal system. They knew it was the perfect source of law. They've indicated it is what makes us a distinctive people. Ultimately, they knew that any society that lives up to that standard is a society that has a shot. But although they never said it, I suspect most of those Founding Fathers knew there was an

YOUR DAILY PHIL

ultimate aim of the law—to teach us how to live together in godly love and peace.

*   *   *

God, thank you for the Bible, which is the perfect source of law. Help me to study your Word and learn how to live with others in godly love and peace.

30

DAY 14 ★ A NEW KIND OF LAW
AND ORDER

**A new command I give you: Love one another.
As I have loved you, so you must love one another.
By this everyone will know that you are my disciples,
if you love one another.**
—JOHN 13:34–35

J esus was clear about his kingship, and he was clear on the laws ordering his kingdom. In fact, he shared the two greatest laws in all the kingdom: love God with everything you have and love your neighbors as yourself (Matt. 22:37–39). He taught that his kingdom was not marked by the politics of power. Instead, he said:

> The kings of the Gentiles lord it over them; and those who exercise authority over them call themselves Benefactors. But you are not to be like that. Instead, the greatest among you should be like the youngest, and the one who rules like the one who serves. For who is greater, the one who is at the table or the one who serves? Is it not the one who is at the table? But I am among you as one who serves. (Luke 22:25–27)

The gospel of John records Jesus' revolutionary law this way: "A new command [or law] I give you: Love one another. As I have loved you, so you must love one another. By this everyone will know that you are my disciples, if you love one another" (13:34–35).

In the eternal kingdom, there was a certain kind of law and order. It was not the law and order that came through passing law after law, through regulating every human behavior. Instead, order in the kingdom comes through practicing love and service. But this begs the question, how exactly did Jesus love and serve others?

31

Jesus healed the lame and lepers, there's no doubt about that. He provided food for the hungry and even a little wine for a wedding where the well had run dry. He met people where they had physical needs, but he never shied away from sharing hard spiritual truths. He called the people to repent by saying, "The kingdom of heaven has come near" (Matt. 4:17). He instructed the woman caught in adultery to "go now and leave your life of sin" (John 8:11). He called the rich to leave their luxuries, the sinners and tax collectors to leave behind their sinful ways, and the religious leaders to leave all their hollow laws. He warned them all: "Unless you repent, you too will all perish" (Luke 13:3).

You see, the law of love provides for both our physical and spiritual needs. It warns of sinful living and godless laws. It calls people to repentance and asks them to live in the kingdom of love. So ask yourself: Do I put my trust in the laws of men or do I live out the kingdom law of love, the law that serves others and invites them to repent?

Lord, I confess that too often I put my trust in the laws of men. Help me to live out your kingdom law of love by serving others and inviting them to repentance today.

DAY 15 ★ SPEAKING THE TRUTH IN LOVE

Speaking the truth in love, we will grow to become in every respect the mature body of him who is the head, that is, Christ.
—EPHESIANS 4:15

I've never been one to run from the truth. Like the Old Testament prophet Jeremiah, the Word of God is shut up in my bones, and I can't hold back (Jer. 20:9). With so much on the line—the souls of men—how could I hold my tongue? So I've preached the Word of Truth to river rats and rednecks. I've preached it to prisoners and politicians. I've even preached it to magazine writers from New York City.

In 2013, at the height of the family's *Duck Dynasty* popularity, I agreed to an interview with one of those city-slicked men's magazines.[1] The interviewer showed up on the river, wanting to talk about my peculiar way of life, my peculiar family, and my peculiar faith.

As I do with almost everyone who comes to visit, I took him to the fields and showed him the work of the Almighty. I showed him the blinds the boys and I had built over the years and gave him a tour of the hunting grounds. I'm sure I told him about the creativity of our God.

When the conversation turned to modern America, I gave it to him straight. We've believed the lies of the Devil, I told him. We've blurred the lines between what's right and wrong and have changed the definition of sin. So it didn't surprise me a lick when he asked, "What, in your mind, is sinful?" But instead of giving him a piece of my own mind, I gave it to him right out of the Scriptures. He'd later quote me as saying,

"Start with homosexual behavior, and just morph out from there. Bestiality, sleeping around with this woman and that woman and that woman and those men. . . . Don't be deceived. Neither the adulterers, the idolaters, the male prostitutes, the homosexual offenders, the greedy, the drunkards, the slanderers, the swindlers—they won't inherit the kingdom of God. Don't deceive yourself. It's not right."[2]

Recognize that list? It's the same list laid out in Paul's letter to the Corinthians (1 Cor. 6:9–10). It's a recitation of the absolute truth of the Scriptures.

Over the course of the day, I'd preach the full truth of God: there is an eternal penalty for sin, the penalty is eternal death, and the Almighty sent Jesus to conquer death so we could live forever with him. I loved that old boy enough to give him the saving truth, but he didn't move on it, at least not on the spot. And when he'd gathered all the material he needed, he loaded his gear and headed back to his suburban life.

I didn't think much more about that interview—that is, until the magazine published the article and the entire world seemed to lose its collective mind. Gay rights groups said I was homophobic and misinformed. A number of folks said I shouldn't be allowed one of the most fundamental protections of the United States Constitution—freedom of speech. To add to it, I found myself suspended indefinitely from appearing on *Duck Dynasty*. All this ruckus, and why? Because I'd spoken the truth of the Bible, the truth of the Almighty.

★　　★　　★

Lord, help me to speak the truth in love, no matter what others may say. Your Word is the only truth that can give eternal life.

DAY 16 ★ THE ULTIMATE TRUTH

For God so loved the world that he gave his
one and only Son, that whoever believes in him
shall not perish but have eternal life.
—JOHN 3:16

Little by little, lie by lie, the lines of morality, decency, and virtue have moved in America. If you'd told me fifty years ago how different America would look today, I wouldn't have believed you. I couldn't have fathomed America's abortion epidemic, wouldn't have thought I'd live in a country where hundreds of thousands of babies are aborted every year. Even though I wasn't really the praying kind, I wouldn't have believed prayer would be pushed out of school. I'd never have imagined so much chaos, so many violent protests or mass shootings. And if you'd told me that in fifty years marriage would no longer be defined as being between a man and a woman, I'd have called you insane.

The enemy of America's soul has come to steal, kill, and destroy (John 10:10). He's slicked us, convinced us generation by generation to take one step further away from the absolute truth of God. How's he done it? He's sold us these ten lies: (1) God is dead; (2) there is no Devil; (3) truth is relative; (4) God did not create life; (5) sex is for self-gratification; (6) virtue is outdated; (7) laws can be ignored or changed if they are inconvenient; (8) unity is not possible; (9) church participation and day-to-day life should be kept separate; and (10) Christians should shut their traps.

But we can return to God if we recognize those lies and live into these truths of the Almighty: (1) the God of the Bible is not dead and he never will be; (2) the Devil of the Bible is real and he is our enemy; (3) there is absolute truth and it comes from God; (4) God is the Author of life and he wants to fulfill it; (5) God created sexuality for his purposes and our good; (6) God's standard for all time is the standard of virtue; (7) law and order come from the Word of God; (8) unity flows from a God-centered culture; (9) the church is God's presence in the day-to-day world, keeping the world from becoming hell on earth; and (10) God's people are his prophetic voice in the world.

These truths aren't just powerful in word. And if we stay true to them, they'll set people free.

This, I suppose, brings me to the ultimate truth: the Almighty loves you, me, and the rest of America. He loves us so much, he sent Jesus to earth to teach us that perfect truth, to live a sinless life, and to conquer sin and death. What's more, he clearly communicated the story of Jesus through the Scriptures. From Genesis to Malachi, the Almighty told us to pay attention because Jesus—the Savior of the world—was coming. From Matthew to John, the writers told us to pay attention because Christ had come. In Acts through Revelation, the writers reminded us that Christ is coming again, and when he comes, he'll honor those who've honored him and punish those who've fallen for the evil one's lies.

God, thank you for the ultimate truth that you love me—and you love America—so much that you sent Jesus to conquer sin and death for us. Help me to live in a way that honors you and to share the truth of the gospel with others.

DAY 17 ★ WE NEED THE KING'S TRUTH

Flee the evil desires of youth and pursue righteousness, faith, love and peace, along with those who call on the Lord out of a pure heart.
—2 TIMOTHY 2:22

How have I seen our country change in these seventy-plus years I've been alive? A good question, I guess. I can remember a day and age when our parents taught us to love God, obey authority, and show respect for the men and women who served this country. We may not have always agreed with the president, but we showed him respect and honor. We pledged allegiance to the flag before school, said a prayer for our country. We did our best to help our neighbors, too, particularly since the federal government wasn't making grand promises of free healthcare or housing or whatever. The country seemed less divided, less fragile. We the People were a family.

Times have changed, though, and if you ask me, it's not been for the best. We've thrown God out of the public arena, legalized abortion, and changed the definition of marriage. We've adopted policies that advance a socialist agenda, policies like free healthcare for all. We worship nature instead of the Creator of that nature. We're on the brink of undoing the Second Amendment. We follow every sexual desire we have. We've seen the disintegration of the home, higher rates of drug addiction and homelessness, and a complete breakdown of the fabric of America. How might I sum it up? Chaos. Lawlessness. Sin runs wild. If I had to describe it in biblical terms, I might call it the end of days.

We're a couple of millennia removed from the writing of the New Testament, but it seems more applicable today than ever. In fact, it seems to describe the present culture of America. Consider Paul's second letter to Timothy, in which he gave the citizens of the kingdom instructions for living in a godless age:

> Flee the evil desires of youth and pursue righteousness, faith, love and peace, along with those who call on the Lord out of a pure heart. Don't have anything to do with foolish and stupid arguments, because you know they produce quarrels. And the Lord's servant must not be quarrelsome but must be kind to everyone, able to teach, not resentful. Opponents must be gently instructed, in the hope that God will grant them repentance leading them to a knowledge of the truth, and that they will come to their senses and escape from the trap of the devil, who has taken them captive to do his will. (2:22–26)

See there? Followers of the King were to chase after the King. Pursue the King. They were to love their neighbors and be kind to them. They were to take the truth of the King to the streets in an effort to save the people from surefire destruction.

★　★　★

King Jesus, I want to pursue you and your kingdom. Give me the courage to take your truth to the streets, so people will come to their senses and escape from the Devil's snare.

DAY 18 ★ WHEN THE FINAL DAY COMES

**But mark this: There will be terrible times in the
last days.**
—2 TIMOTHY 3:1

What happens when a nation turns its back on God's truth? Pay attention to Paul's prophecy:

> But mark this: There will be terrible times in the last days. People
> will be lovers of themselves, lovers of money, boastful, proud, abu-
> sive, disobedient to their parents, ungrateful, unholy, without love,
> unforgiving, slanderous, without self-control, brutal, not lovers of
> the good, treacherous, rash, conceited, lovers of pleasure rather than
> lovers of God—having a form of godliness but denying its power.
> Have nothing to do with such people.
>
> They are the kind who worm their way into homes and gain
> control over gullible women, who are loaded down with sins and
> are swayed by all kinds of evil desires, always learning but never
> able to come to a knowledge of the truth. . . . They are men of
> depraved minds, who, as far as the faith is concerned, are rejected.
> (2 Tim. 3:1–8)

Sound familiar? Start down the list Paul wrote out and ask yourself: *Does that list describe our current political candidates? Are they
lovers of themselves, lovers of money, boastful, proud, and sometimes
abusive? Are they unholy, unforgiving, slanderous, without self-control,
or lovers of good? Are they treacherous, rash, conceited? Do they love
pleasure and power more than the Almighty? Do they genuinely love
their neighbors?*

And what did Paul say about the end of these sorts of people? In
his letter to the Philippians, he wrote: "For, as I have often told you

before and now tell you again even with tears, many live as enemies of the cross of Christ. Their destiny is destruction" (3:18–19).

If I'm honest, I'd say the current political landscape in America looks a lot like the last days Paul described, the days that will inevitably lead to destruction. In fact, it's uncanny. Maybe even surreal. But here's the truth that should bring us great comfort, and it comes right out of the Scriptures:

> Why do the nations conspire
>> and the peoples plot in vain?
> The kings of the earth rise up
>> and the rulers band together
>> against the LORD and against his anointed, saying,
> "Let us break their chains
>> and throw off their shackles."
>
> The One enthroned in heaven laughs;
>> the Lord scoffs at them.
> He rebukes them in his anger
>> and terrifies them in his wrath, saying,
> "I have installed my king
>> on Zion, my holy mountain." (Psalm 2:1–6)

Yes, American politicians can do all their plotting and scheming. They can pretend they're in control, that they know better than the Almighty, that they can somehow free us from his rules for living, maybe lead us into a more progressive, scientific, utopian future. They can change the laws to suit their desires and chase the sin of the day. They can try to kill God, ignore him, or deny his kingdom, but no matter how hard they try, they cannot stand against the one true King: King Jesus.

And when the final day comes, when King Jesus returns, I want to be found worthy. I want to be found carrying his standard. Loving people the way he would. Letting my faith lead my time, talent, resources, and my vote. I want to be found at his side, laughing alongside him at the hollow schemes of men.

King Jesus, others may try to ignore you or deny you, but I know that you alone are the way, the truth, and the life. May I be faithful to your Word so that when the final day comes, I will be found worthy.

DAY 19 ★ SO WHAT CAN YOU DO?

We must pay the most careful attention,
therefore, to what we have heard,
so that we do not drift away.
—HEBREWS 2:1

If we don't change course, America is headed toward chaos and destruction. If we keep chasing our desires and entitlements, if we keep passing laws that call evil good and good evil, we'll find ourselves wrapping up this constitutional experiment, sure enough. But no matter which course the American political system takes, those who turn their eyes to the King and trust in his saving power will be spared from the surefire destruction that's coming.

Yes, we know destruction is coming, and even if it's not in this decade, humankind can't escape it forever. The writer of the letter to the Hebrews assures us that even in the face of that destruction, there is a way of escape:

> In the past God spoke to our ancestors through the prophets at many times and in various ways, but in these last days he has spoken to us by his Son, whom he appointed heir of all things, and through whom also he made the universe. (1:1–2)

As if to make himself even more clear, the writer continued:

> But about the Son he says, "Your throne . . . will last for ever and ever; a scepter of justice will be the scepter of your kingdom." (v. 8)

Jesus, the heir of all things, the radiance of God's glory, the one who sits on the throne and holds the scepter of justice over his kingdom is the King who provided a way of escape. And that being the case, the author of Hebrews instructed us:

> We must pay the most careful attention, therefore, to what we have heard, so that we do not drift away. For since the message spoken through angels was binding, and every violation and disobedience received its just punishment, how shall we escape if we ignore so great a salvation? This salvation, which was first announced by the Lord, was confirmed to us by those who heard him. God also testified to it by signs, wonders and various miracles, and by gifts of the Holy Spirit distributed according to his will. (2:1–4)

The sad truth is that America hasn't paid careful attention to the truth we once knew. We've strayed from the truth we once held so dear. But even if our country continues on its slow slide to disobedience and punishment, even if we continue toward destruction at breakneck speed, there's good news for the followers of the King. We can be saved, even if our democracy, our country, or even our environment burns to the ground. Yes, the world might grind to a halt, but our salvation is secure if we follow the King. I know, because the Bible says as much.

The prophet Isaiah assured us that the whole world (which includes its political systems) is on the way to winding down. He wrote:

> All the stars in the sky will be dissolved
> > and the heavens rolled up like a scroll;
> all the starry hosts will fall
> > like withered leaves from the vine,
> > like shriveled figs from the fig tree. (Isa. 34:4)

Still, the people were not to worry. Why? Because even though all the systems of the world perish, the King was on the scene, and he promised,

> My salvation will last forever,
>> my righteousness will never fail. (51:6)

★　　★　　★

Lord, even if all the systems of this world perish, I will still trust in you. Thank you for your promise that my salvation is secure if I follow the King.

DAY 20 ★ LIVE OUT THE TRUTH

Since everything will be destroyed in this way, what kind of people ought you to be? You ought to live holy and godly lives as you look forward to the day of God and speed its coming.
—2 PETER 3:11-12

The writers of the New Testament knew that the nations, government systems, and the world itself were headed toward the final judgment. Paul wrote:

> The time is short. From now on those who have wives should live as if they do not; those who mourn, as if they did not; those who are happy, as if they were not; those who buy something, as if it were not theirs to keep; those who use the things of the world, as if not engrossed in them. For this world in its present form is passing away. (1 Cor. 7:29–31)

But just because the world was passing away didn't mean there was no hope. The followers of the King were given a specific charge. Paul put it this way: "We fix our eyes not on what is seen, but on what is unseen, since what is seen is temporary, but what is unseen is eternal" (2 Cor. 4:18).

Peter shared about the coming end of the age too. But he didn't stop there. He wrote about how the citizens of the King should live as that end approached:

> But the day of the Lord will come like a thief. The heavens will disappear with a roar; the elements will be destroyed by fire, and the earth and everything done in it will be laid bare.
>
> Since everything will be destroyed in this way, what kind of people ought you to be? You ought to live holy and godly lives as

you look forward to the day of God and speed its coming. . . . But in keeping with his promise we are looking forward to a new heaven and a new earth, where righteousness dwells. (2 Peter 3:10–13)

And if this advice wasn't specific enough, he added:

Since you are looking forward to this, make every effort to be found spotless, blameless and at peace with him. Bear in mind that our Lord's patience means salvation, just as our dear brother Paul also wrote you with the wisdom that God gave him. (vv. 14–15)

John also shared about the passing nature of the world as compared to the eternal promises of God: "The world and its desires pass away, but whoever does the will of God lives forever" (1 John 2:17).

So, America, as we continue down the path of degradation and destruction, I'll keep preaching the truth. I'll keep sharing with the hope that our country will turn away from sin and plot a course back to the Almighty, the King of kings. I'll vote in ways that protect our freedoms, our religious liberty, and that give us the best chance to return to the King. But even if our country doesn't correct its course, even if we continue on this slow slide to the coming destruction, I'll do my best to live a life that's godly. I'll do my best to bring as many along as I can too.

I hope you'll make the same commitments. I hope you'll support candidates who follow the King and vote for policies in line with his causes. More than that, though, I hope you'll live out the King's mandates. I hope you'll preach and teach the good news of the King wherever you go and live a life worthy of the coming salvation.

★　　★　　★

King Jesus, even though our nation is on a course of degradation and destruction, I want to live a life that honors you. Help me to live out your truth and share your good news of salvation wherever I go.

★ PART II ★

FREEDOM

IT IS FOR FREEDOM THAT CHRIST HAS
SET US FREE. STAND FIRM, THEN, AND
DO NOT LET YOURSELVES BE BURDENED
AGAIN BY A YOKE OF SLAVERY.

—GALATIANS 5:1

DAY 21 ★ A TASTE FOR FREEDOM

They promise them freedom, while they themselves are slaves of depravity—for "people are slaves to whatever has mastered them."
—2 PETER 2:19

Miss Kay and I met while I was in high school. I genuinely loved her and wanted to spend the rest of my life with her. So, when we discovered Miss Kay was pregnant with our first child, Al, we had what we referred to as a "pioneer wedding" in the summer of 1964.

I'd been offered a scholarship to play on the football team at Louisiana Tech University. So Miss Kay and I packed up what little we had and made our way to Ruston, Louisiana. The sixties were in full swing when we arrived on campus; it was the height of the hippie movement. My professors had concluded that God was dead, so man was free. Free to party. Free to join the sexual revolution. Free to chase happiness.

Because I'd never heard the good news of the living God, I began to buy what these professors were selling. If God was dead, shouldn't I be free to chase my own happiness?

I graduated college by the skin of my teeth in 1969 and entered the master of education program at Louisiana Tech. That fall I began teaching English and coaching sports in Junction City, Arkansas, while I took my master's classes at night. At Junction City I met Big Al Bolen on the first day of school. He was a large man with an even larger intellect, and his appetite for a good party was even larger still. I was drawn to the kind of freedom he seemed to embody, and he invited me into his rowdy lifestyle.

We'd teach during the day and raise hell during the night. On the weekends we'd be the last ones out of the bar. We'd meet up with a small band of miscreants just off the beaten path, and we'd get high, get drunk, and get laid, mostly in that order. I did it all despite the fact that I was a husband and a father.

For the first time I was tasting what I thought was freedom—the drugs, the drinking, the sleeping around. With each passing night I indulged a little more. For a time that indulgence felt so good. It was a lifestyle I'd never experienced, but as is the Robertson way, I took to it like a duck to water.

As the years wore on, my behavior became more erratic and unruly. I was losing control. On many occasions I'd come through the trailer door after a night of partying, and there'd be Miss Kay, tending the children and waiting on me. So often I'd shift the blame; I'd light into her and accuse her of her own infidelities, of sleeping around. The irony was not lost on her, and she'd protest, tell me that she was too busy working and raising our boys to cheat. She was trying her best to hold the family together, she said. What's more, she knew I was guilty of my own indiscretions, and she did not shy away from confronting me.

"Why are you acting this way? Why don't you come home and be with your family?"

"I just need my freedom," I told her.

"Is this freedom? Really?"

Miss Kay was right. I didn't know what true freedom was.

Lord, everywhere I look, it seems the world is telling me that I need freedom—freedom to be anyone and do anything I want. Help me to understand that true freedom comes from you.

DAY 22 ★ THE PRISON OF FALSE FREEDOM

The righteous hate what is false,
but the wicked make themselves a stench
and bring shame on themselves.
—PROVERBS 13:5

My days of debauchery reached their height in 1975. I'd lost my job as a high school teacher the year before. As if that wasn't enough, I'd managed a bar after that stint as a high school teacher and coach. And though it'd been a successful business venture, I'd lost it all in a violent dispute and resulting fist fight with the property owners. The owners had shuttered the bar. They'd pressed charges too. I went on the run.

A fugitive from the law, I was flat broke. Needing employment, I took a job on an offshore rig in the Gulf of Mexico, and in the between times, I hid out in the woods and partied with Big Al and the gang while Miss Kay sorted out my legal troubles. I was shirking responsibilities, controlled by my own desires. The desire to drink. The desire for women. The desire to do what I wanted to do. But the more I chased my desires, the emptier I felt. And with this realization, a deep guilt set in.

The guilt was the thing that led to my outburst with Miss Kay one night in the trailer that led to her leaving. It was the source of my fury, my anger, even my jealousy. Thinking it was my family who caused all the guilt, who kept me from experiencing ultimate freedom, I could only see one solution. I had to get rid of them. Maybe by pushing them away, I thought, I'd push the guilt away too.

After Miss Kay pulled away from the trailer in her VW, I decided to make the most of my newfound freedom. I'd live it up. I'd work when I wanted, hunt and fish when I wanted. I'd drink what I wanted, when I wanted, and with whomever I wanted. For a week or so I did just that. I lived in my own bachelor's paradise. But it didn't take long for the truth to set in: my ideal bachelor's paradise was no kind of paradise at all. In fact, it was a prison of guilt, shame, and loneliness. Why didn't I feel a new sense of freedom? What had gone wrong?

God, so many of the things I think will make me happy lead only to a prison of guilt, shame, and loneliness. Whenever I'm tempted to listen to the Devil's lies, remind me of your true freedom.

DAY 23 ★ A NEW KIND OF FREEDOM

If the Son sets you free, you will be free indeed.
—JOHN 8:36

I ran up on Miss Kay while I was still living under my parents' strict moral code. I was sixteen, and she was two years my junior, and I knew from the start that she was the one for me. We took to each other like ducks to water—analogy intended—and whenever I had any free time, I spent it with Miss Kay. We dated through our high school years, and just before college, we were married and had our first son, Alan. But as I began to enjoy success on the football field at Louisiana Tech, I started partying more and more with my teammates, often without Miss Kay, who was too busy rearing little Al. The partying gave me a taste of freedom, a taste of what it meant to chase my own desires like a Labrador puppy might chase its own tail.

Come to find out, if you chase your tail long enough, you'll catch it.

For the next several years, I spiraled down into my own desires, into booze and pills and easy women. The hippie movement was on, and though I was no hippie, I enjoyed the fruits of their sexual revolution, all the while leaving Miss Kay at home to tend to the children by herself. By the time Miss Kay left me, I'm sorry to say I was a regular whoremonger. And without Miss Kay to stand in the way of my sexual appetite, I did what I wanted, with whom I wanted, and I did it all in the name of freedom. All that sex wasn't freedom at all, though. It didn't satisfy my itch for long, and only left me with guilt, shame, and a suffocating loneliness. It was, of course, that guilt, shame, and loneliness that drove me back to the arms of Miss Kay, and ultimately into the arms of the Almighty.

Guilt and shame have their purpose, see.

When I heard the good news of Jesus, when I realized he'd freed me from all my sins and given me a new life, both now and in eternity, everything changed. In that change, some things didn't need to be explained by the preacher. I knew my days of lawbreaking were over. I knew my days of drinking and getting high had come to an end. I knew it was time to rededicate myself to God-honoring work, to building something that would provide for my family, church, and community. More than anything, though, I knew my personal sexual revolution was over. I was finished running around on Miss Kay.

I dedicated myself to the truth of the Scriptures and learned there really were moral absolutes. Time and time again, the Scriptures warned against the kind of sexual immorality that had so marked my life. As I learned to walk in the light of God's Word instead of the darkness of my own desire, I found I was making an easy trade. Sexual purity and dedication to Miss Kay were more satisfying than all the sexual freedom in the world. Fifty years later, I can tell you this: I haven't missed those days of debauchery for a minute.

Jesus, thank you for the good news of salvation, which frees us from sin and gives us new life! Help me to walk in the light of God's Word instead of the darkness of my own desires.

DAY 24 ★ NEVER TOO LATE
FOR FREEDOM

I am sending you to them to open their eyes and turn them from darkness to light, and from the power of Satan to God, so that they may receive forgiveness of sins and a place among those who are sanctified by faith in me.
—ACTS 26:17–18

Twelve years after my conversion, the phone rang.

"I need to talk with you."

It was Big Al.

"Can you come up to Junction City?"

I hung up the phone and told Miss Kay that I thought his time had come. I drove to Arkansas and met him on the banks of the river. "I've been keeping up with you," Al said, "and I've never seen such a change in a man." He kicked at the pine needles on the ground and then said, "Guess what my doctor told me?"

"What?" I asked.

"I have an aneurysm in my heart that could burst at any moment."

I asked, "So, are you having second thoughts about your atheism?"

Big Al nodded, then asked me what had made such a difference in my life. How had I changed? I relayed my conversion story, shared how I'd been a prisoner of the Devil and how God had freed me from that prison. I shared the death, burial, and resurrection of Jesus and the death, burial, and resurrection of Phil Robertson. I told him that the Devil had enslaved him through his own desires, but that God wanted to free him from that bondage. I gave him the unfiltered truth of God, shared the good news of Jesus with him, and when I was finished, I waited for his response.

"I tell you what," he said, "because of this aneurysm, I don't know

55

if I'm going to make it. This story, if it's true, it changes everything. I reckon I underestimated it."

That was an understatement.

"Think you could take me down to the river and baptize me?"

"Yes," I said, and that's just what we did.

Two months later I received a call from Big Al's wife. He was gone. Before he passed he'd requested me to preach at his funeral. So I showed up. Come to find out, Big Al had become quite the figure in Junction City, and it was a packed house.

"Let me tell you a story about Al," I said. "A couple of months ago, I had the privilege of baptizing Al into the family of Christ." I shared the story, and I laid out the good news of Jesus. I told them that Jesus wanted to set them free, just like he had Al. Before leaving the stage, I looked down in the casket and said, "My old buddy, I'll see you again."

Al, the staunchest atheist I'd ever met, had unwound the lies of the Devil before the end. He'd been freed from Satan's power, freed from the power of death too. He'd become a child of God.

Big Al could be a testament to America. Sure, we might be tangled up in the Devil's lies. We might celebrate violence and drunkenness and sex and drugs, success, wealth, scientific advancement—anything really. But if we come to see that without Jesus we're on the road to eternal death—just as I did, just as Big Al did—we can come into a new season of freedom. That freedom, though, won't come without an awakening, without an infusion of absolute truth, and this is the absolute truth—the real and living God wants to free us from death; he wants to free us to flourish.

★   ★   ★

Lord, you are the living God who wants to set us free from death and give us eternal life in heaven with you. Help me to be aware of the opportunities you are giving me to share the gospel of your salvation.

DAY 25 ★ THE TEMPTATION TO BE FREE OF GOD

The serpent said to the woman, "You will not surely die. For God knows that when you eat of it your eyes will be opened, and you will be like God, knowing good and evil."
—GENESIS 3:4–5 ESV

The world tries to convince us that the Devil is dead, but it's a specious argument, one based on circular reasoning. Both Scripture and my own personal experience undercut this argument. Truth is, my life attests: Satan, the father of all lies, the chief prevaricator, is very much alive. Truth is, he'd rather have you believe that he's dead, inactive, or a myth if it'd keep you out of the arms of God.

The question of God—who first posed it? You know the story of Genesis, how God planted a garden and set a man named Adam in the middle of it. From Adam's rib he cut a woman and named her Eve. As the story goes, God gave Adam and Eve full rule over the garden, with only one restriction. They could not eat of the tree in the center of the garden, the Tree of the Knowledge of Good and Evil. If they did, God said, they would die. Seems simple enough, right?

Enter the Devil.

Taking the form of a serpent, the vile liar visited Eve and tempted her first with a question: "God told you not to eat from that tree?" Eve responded and said God had warned them that if they ate from the tree, mankind would be finished. That's when the first lie entered the ears of a human. "The serpent said to the woman, 'You will not surely die. For God knows that when you eat of it your eyes will be opened, and you will be like God, knowing good and evil'" (Gen. 3:4–5 ESV). You can set yourself free of God, the Devil intimated; you can kill him and become your own god.

Sound familiar?

Eve was tricked by the Devil's lies, and what was the result of that trick? Sin entered the world, and with it, an endless cycle of death and destruction. Into the world came drunkenness. Into the world came sexual immorality and perversion. Into the world came wars and rumors of wars. Into the world came violence and racial divide. The world was forever changed because of the crafty lies spun by a slithering serpent. Those lies have slithered on throughout history.

In the Gospels that record the life of Jesus, we see the Devil, still scheming, still spinning the same sorts of lies, still tempting people with the lie that life would be so much better if we could only be free of God.

In the eighth chapter of John, Jesus was speaking to the people, and some religious leaders were in the crowd. Jesus—a man known for saying it like it was—spoke the truth, said that every last one of them had been born into sin slavery. Jesus outed the truth. The Devil was alive and active, and he controlled the desires of the religious leaders of the day.

There was good news, though. He'd come to bring freedom, and if they followed his command, they'd be free indeed.

Jesus, thank you for coming to this world and exposing the Devil's lies. The enemy of our souls tempts us to become our own god, but you came to reveal that you alone can set us free.

DAY 26 ★ THE FREEDOM TO LOVE ONE ANOTHER

A new command I give you: Love one another.
As I have loved you, so you must love one another.
—JOHN 13:34

These days it seems like so many are out for themselves. They've forgotten how to sacrifice their own desires for the good of their fellow man. This is what the virtue of biblical charity is all about—sacrificial love. Did anyone do this better than Christ, the man who gave his life to pay for our sins? Consider his most charitable command: "A new command I give you: Love one another. As I have loved you, so you must love one another" (John 13:34). Do you think a love like Jesus', one that gives of itself for the sake of the world, would make a difference in America? I do.

The Scriptures have plenty to say about the virtuous life. They speak to being sober, wise managers of money, hardworking, just, kind, and loving, both to men and God. The Devil would have us believe the lie that these virtues are outdated, and the result is nothing short of chaos. As proof, you only need to look to those politicians under his control. Don't they love their uncivil speech, mocking and insulting each other at every turn? Don't they mismanage money, running up our deficit year after year? Aren't so many of them caught in sexual scandals, unable to be self-controlled and sober? And what about the people of this country? Don't we resemble our politicians?

Consider it: If we lived a life of virtue as described in the Bible, wouldn't it change the course of our country? Wouldn't our opioid epidemic, our drunkenness, and the effects of our sexual immorality be a distant memory if we practiced self-control? Wouldn't our hard work and frugality save us from the burdens of a welfare state and maybe lead to a reduction of our national debt? Wouldn't we be kinder to one another, only saying things that would help each other? Wouldn't the chaotic violence spilling into the streets stop if we were committed to justice, civility, and loving one another?

You bet.

American Christian: you have the responsibility to be a model of virtue. Be salt and light. Only through godly virtue can the people of God bring heaven to earth. Who doesn't want that?

Jesus, help me to demonstrate your love and be a model of virtue to others. May my civility, wisdom, and kindness make a real difference in the lives of my family, my friends, and my nation.

DAY 27 ★ THE VALUE OF VIRTUE

**His divine power has given us everything we need
for a godly life through our knowledge of him who
called us by his own glory and goodness.**
—2 PETER 1:3

Our Founding Fathers knew the value of virtue. Consider Ben Franklin, who tried his best to live by thirteen virtues, including the following six:

1. Silence—"Speak not but what may benefit others or yourself; avoid trifling conversation"
2. Frugality—"Make no expense but to do good to others or yourself; waste nothing"
3. Industry—"Lose no time; be always employ'd in something useful; cut off all unnecessary actions"
4. Justice—"Wrong none by doing injuries, or omitting the benefits that are your duty"
5. Tranquility—"Be not disturbed at trifles, or at accidents common or unavoidable"
6. Humility—"Imitate Jesus and Socrates"[1]

What's more, he knew the source and supremacy of those virtues and morals, stating, "As to Jesus of Nazareth, my opinion of whom you particularly desire, I think the system of morals and His religion as He left them to us, the best the world ever saw or is likely to see."[2]

Likewise, our first president, George Washington, knew virtue and morality couldn't exist without the influence of God. In his farewell address of 1796, Washington said, "Whatever may be conceded to the influence of refined education on minds of peculiar structure—reason & experience both forbid us to expect that National morality can prevail in exclusion of religious principle."[3] What religious principle did he mean? Of virtue and character he wrote, "To the distinguished Character of Patriot, it should be our highest Glory to add the more distinguished Character of Christian."[4]

John Adams—Founding Father, first vice president, and second president—chimed in too, knowing that without God our society would spin into virtueless chaos. He wrote, "Without Religion, this World would be Something not fit to be mentioned in polite Company: I mean Hell."[5] And if a world without religion would be hell, what would be its opposite? In his diary entry dated February 22, 1756, Adams wrote:

> Suppose a nation in some distant region should take the Bible for their only law book, and every member should regulate his conduct by the precepts there exhibited. Every member would be obliged in conscience to temperance and frugality and industry, to justice and kindness and charity towards his fellow men, and to piety and love and reverence toward almighty God. . . . What a Eutopia, what a Paradise would this region be.[6]

In other words, Adams believed that if our country relied on the Scriptures, if we allowed the Bible to regulate our government and its citizens, we would live in a more virtuous civilization. We'd be sober, frugal, hardworking, law-abiding, kind, generous, reverent, and loving people. Doesn't that sound like the kind of country you'd want to live in? It sounds like the closest thing to heaven we could experience this side of death if you ask me.

The Founding Fathers knew that a virtueless society could not prosper. They knew that without virtues we'd slide into corruption, laziness, incivility, and ultimately chaos.

★   ★   ★

God, you have given us everything we need to live godly lives. May America return to the virtues based on your Word, and may my life be an example of those virtues you desire.

DAY 28 ★ OUR NEED FOR BIBLICAL VIRTUE

Join together in following my example, brothers
and sisters, and just as you have us as a model,
keep your eyes on those who live as we do.
—PHILIPPIANS 3:17

While filming *Duck Dynasty,* I had the privilege of meeting some New York City muckety-mucks in the entertainment industry. From time to time they'd come down to West Monroe to spend time with Miss Kay and me. They wanted to get to know us, to see whether we were the real deal. We'd put on a big pot of duck gumbo or jambalaya or crawfish étouffée, and we'd sit around the table and talk.

Sitting across the table from one of those executives, I asked whether I could hazard a guess as to how *Duck Dynasty* had found its way to their network. The way I figured it, I said, a group of executives like him were sitting around a table, and one of them proposed filming a reality show about a functional, hardworking family that'd made a name for themselves. I reckoned they needed a family of character and full of characters, one without a hint of scandal. I took it a step further and guessed that someone in that room had asked, "Where will we find a family like that?"

I paused and asked if I had it about right.

He was smiling, nodding along.

"And then you found a bunch of decent river rats making duck calls down here in Northern Louisiana, and you were all intrigued. Am I close?"

"That's about it," he said.

"How's that worked out for you?" I asked.

He just smiled.

During the *Duck Dynasty* years, I'm sure there were some viewers who tuned in for the novelty of a bunch of Bible-thumping, shotgun-tote'n, beard-wear'n, duck-call-make'n dudes who'd married virtuous women way above their pay grades. I reckon some of those viewers found our practice of biblical virtues peculiar. But as they watched, they witnessed a family committed to living a life of biblical virtue. They saw how that kind of family enjoys stability, peace of mind, family order, and prosperity. In short, they saw the fruit of living by the Almighty's commands. And if the ratings were any indication, they were hungry for it.

The American people are mired in an unprecedented time of instability, incivility, and regular chaos. Their families are broken. Kindness is in short supply. They'll lie, cheat, and steal, or be hurt by those who lie, cheat, or steal. Why? Simple. America has fallen for the enemy's lie, the lie that biblical virtues are outdated.

Without virtue America has no moral authority, and without moral authority can we survive? I don't think so. But where will we turn to learn virtues?

The entertainment industry in Hollywood, California? No way.

The news desks in New York City? Nope.

The politicians and policy makers in Washington, DC? Nah.

There's only one source of true virtue, a source that's been time-tested—the Bible. Its code is simple and true: don't be a drunkard or drug addict; spend your money wisely; work hard; promote justice and law and order; be kind to others, always civil; love your neighbor. Friend, if you'd save yourself, turn from the lie of the evil one, trust Jesus, and commit yourself to the truth of biblical virtue. If you do, you'll inspire others to follow suit, and if enough people follow along, maybe we'll find our way to heaven on earth.

*   *   *

God, your Word is the timeless source of all truth. Help me to commit to a life of biblical virtue, so that my example may inspire others to experience the fruit of living by your commands.

DAY 29 ★ THE FREEDOM TO USE CAPITAL FOR THE KING

Whoever is kind to the poor lends to the LORD,
and he will reward them for what they have done.
—PROVERBS 19:17

Y ou might argue capitalism is its own sort of -ism, and in the hands of godless people, it can be just as destructive. True enough. But ask yourself, *Which philosophy—capitalism or socialism—gives the citizens of the kingdom the best opportunity to use their money to advance the causes of the King?* The one that allows a godless government to distribute wealth as they see fit or the system that gives kingdom people the freedom to direct their resources toward godly causes?

Do I really need to ask?

The King could have come and set up a holy socialist government that redistributed wealth to the poor. But if you examine the Scriptures, you'll see that's not what happened. Instead, the King entrusted his people with money and asked them to use it in ways that honored the King.

Throughout the Bible, the Almighty affirms private wealth creation. In the book of Proverbs, Solomon wrote, "Lazy hands make for poverty, but diligent hands bring wealth" (10:4).

In the book of Deuteronomy, Moses handed down the economic policy statement of the Almighty (among other policy statements and laws, of course). Throughout the book, the Almighty seemed to affirm the private ownership of wealth, and he directed his people to use it freely to help others. Consider his version of privatized welfare:

> If anyone is poor among your fellow Israelites in any of the towns of
> the land the LORD your God is giving you, do not be hardhearted

or tightfisted toward them. Rather, be openhanded and freely lend them whatever they need. . . . Give generously to them and do so without a grudging heart; then because of this the LORD your God will bless you in all your work and in everything you put your hand to. There will always be poor people in the land. Therefore I command you to be openhanded toward your fellow Israelites who are poor and needy in your land. (15:7–8, 10–11)

In the same way, God's people are meant to use their resources to employ those in need. Again, in Deuteronomy, Moses shared the Almighty's fair-wage policy:

Do not take advantage of a hired worker who is poor and needy, whether that worker is a fellow Israelite or a foreigner residing in one of your towns. Pay them their wages each day before sunset, because they are poor and are counting on it. (24:14–15)

The theme of using personal wealth to care for the poor continues throughout the Scriptures. Solomon wrote,

- "Whoever oppresses the poor shows contempt for their Maker, but whoever is kind to the needy honors God" (Prov. 14:31).
- "Whoever is kind to the poor lends to the LORD, and he will reward them for what they have done" (Prov. 19:17).
- "The generous will themselves be blessed, for they share their food with the poor" (Prov. 22:9).
- "Those who give to the poor will lack nothing, but those who close their eyes to them receive many curses" (Prov. 28:27).

★   ★   ★

King Jesus, thank you for the money you have entrusted to me. May I be faithful to use it in ways that honor you, help others, and advance your kingdom.

DAY 30 ★ IN PRISON, YET FREE

Where the Spirit of the Lord is, there is freedom.
—2 CORINTHIANS 3:17

Angola, a prison about twenty miles north of St. Francisville, Louisiana, serves as the home of murderers, rapists, and thieves. It has a dedicated death row. As of last count, more than five thousand inmates were behind its razor-wired walls.

I'd been invited to Angola by warden Burl Cain, a man who knew the power of Christ could change the lives of his inmates. When I arrived, Warden Cain invited me to the guesthouse, where he told me that many of the men in these walls would never see the outside. They'd come here to die. But still he believed the gospel of Jesus could give these lawbreakers great hope. He'd seen men in Angola accept the gospel and become reformed. That's why he'd invited me, he said. Several of these men watched *Duck Dynasty*, and maybe they'd listen to the gospel if it was preached by a celebrity. With that he led me to chapel where the inmates gathered.

There in front of the roughest crowd I'd ever seen, I told those men I knew why they were there. They were murderers, rapists, thieves. They had disobeyed God's laws, had broken the Ten Commandments that served as the basis of American law.

"Gentlemen, this is the end of the line for most of you," I said. "Most of you are going to die in this prison, but I have some good news for you. You can be under lock and key, but you can still be free."

I went on to share the good news that if they renounced their law-breaking ways and followed Christ, they could be set free from the sin and shame of their heinous acts. What's more, they could have eternal life.

I closed my gospel presentation, and the men were dismissed. The warden brought in another group. Then another. I shared the good news of Jesus with every man who came through those chapel doors.

In the days after I visited, I'd come to find out that more than a few men had accepted the good news. They'd come to a saving knowledge of Jesus and had been baptized. Their law-breaking records had been wiped clean in the eyes of the Almighty. They'd been set free, even if they couldn't avoid the consequences of their actions. Even if some of them might be executed for their crimes, when they awoke to the afterlife, they would be in a heavenly eternity.

Ironic as it is, all those Angola lawbreakers who accepted the good news of Jesus have found true freedom. So many outside of prisons, though, those who've disobeyed God's laws regarding marriage or abortion or smoking weed or cutting corners to make a little more money, are anything but free. Try as they might to blur the lines of the law, to change the laws that don't suit their pleasures, they can't avoid the punishment coming their way. If they asked, I'd tell them that judgment is coming to them, just as surely as it's come to those in Angola. I'd tell them that the prisons like Angola are a veritable garden of Eden compared to the eternal prison that waits for them. I'd also tell them this: they can be set free from the judgment, just like those brothers in Angola.

★　　★　　★

Lord Jesus, thank you for the good news of the gospel, which sets us free from sin and gives us eternal life. I praise you for providing true freedom, no matter our circumstances.

DAY 31 ★ UNIFIED AND FREE

**Make every effort to keep the unity of the
Spirit through the bond of peace.**
—EPHESIANS 4:3

America is divided. Even a C+ man like me can see as much.

We divide along political lines. (Are you a Republican or Democrat?)

We point out the different economic classes. (Are you working class or a white-collar fella?)

We increasingly divide along racial and gender lines. (Do I even need to explain that one?)

There doesn't seem to be any common ground these days. Instead of peace and harmony, there's nothing but discord, division, and protest. There's racial violence, and class warfare, and gender strife. We're yard dogs, all at each other's throats.

When the Founding Fathers set the stakes of America, they envisioned something less divided, something more unified. They envisioned a society where men and women came together under a single truth. They memorialized this truth in the Declaration of Independence, writing:

> We hold these truths to be self-evident, that all men are created equal, that they are endowed by their Creator with certain unalienable Rights, that among these are Life, Liberty and the Pursuit of Happiness.

The founding ideal of America was that the very real and living God had made all men the same, and he wanted us to be free. He wanted us to share rights, to be unified under his truth, and to be happy, happy, happy.

There's no doubt that our forefathers didn't follow this ideal perfectly, especially in their enactment of laws. They didn't end slavery when they declared independence, and they participated in a land grab from the Native Americans. They had different ideas of what *liberty* meant, too, and they divided into political parties almost as soon as the country was founded. But still, from the very beginning, they hoped for a society that would be unified under the principles in the Declaration of Independence. They hoped for a country where folks worked together to build an equal, virtuous, and ultimately prosperous society.

How'd we get derailed? The enemy, the father of lies, sneaked in and told us this whopper: unity is not possible. All people are not created equal, he said. He's preyed on our differences—religious, political, economic, racial, and gender. He's made us believe that true equality is impossible, convinced us that the only way to get what we deserve is to divide and conquer. And in pointing out our divisions, the enemy of our souls and our country has sowed the seeds of chaos, violence, and even murder.

God, thank you for creating all people to be equal and free. Help our nation recognize the destructive lies of the enemy and return to the unity that comes from our equality in Christ.

DAY 32 ★ INDIVIDUAL LIBERTIES

Therefore, each of you must put off falsehood
and speak truthfully to your neighbor, for
we are all members of one body.
—EPHESIANS 4:25

The Founding Fathers knew the importance of individual liberties. They believed all Americans should enjoy the freedom to practice their religion, the freedom to gather together as people of faith, and the freedom to share what they believe through free speech. What's more, our forefathers believed these liberties were granted to all men by God as natural rights, rights that couldn't be taken away by any government. As Thomas Jefferson noted, "Can the liberties of a nation be thought secure when we have removed their only firm basis, a conviction . . . that these liberties are of the gift of God?"[1]

Nope.

This being the case, they took measures to limit the government's interference with these liberties by including these words in the United States Constitution: "Congress shall make no law respecting an establishment of religion, or prohibiting the free exercise thereof; or abridging the freedom of speech."

In their infinite wisdom, our forefathers hoped to protect us from some future tyrannical government that might try to remove these liberties. They also knew that if individual liberties were to be scaled back, it would most likely start with the erosion of freedom of speech. In fact, Ben Franklin wrote, "The Security of Property, and the Freedom of Speech always go together. . . . Whoever would overthrow the Liberty of a Nation, must begin by subduing the Freeness of Speech."[2]

Ultimately, the Founding Fathers knew that America would be on shaky ground if we removed the right of godly citizens to speak the truth. Freedom of speech was a foundational liberty, and if protected it would allow the citizens to protect all other liberties, liberties like the freedom to practice religion. They also knew that if free speech eroded, America would slide into chaos and tyranny.

Freedom of speech is under attack these days, especially if it's the speech of Christians. Don't believe me? Try speaking about sexuality—or any manner of sin, for that matter—in the public square, the public school, or the public courthouse. If you do, prepare yourself. You'll be called bigoted and hateful. Folks will threaten you with hate-speech legislation. And even if they don't, they'll ridicule you, call you outdated, tell you to shut your trap. Why? It's simple. The American masses killed God, the granter of true liberty, and now they've fallen for this lie of the enemy: freedom of speech shouldn't apply to religious speech, especially when that religious speech touches on issues of sin. Sin speech is called hate speech.

It doesn't take much to imagine America's slide into tyranny, especially if it's tyranny against Bible-believing folks. But should the day come when the tyranny of the masses takes hold of this country, when the lie of the evil one becomes a legislated prohibition on sharing our faith, what's our responsibility?

- To keep speaking the truth anyway.
- To combat the lies of the enemy with the Word of God.
- To expose sin with our words.
- To tell the world of the coming consequences of that sin.
- To share the rescue that came through Jesus.

★   ★   ★

God, thank you that our Founding Fathers recognized the importance of individual liberties, especially freedom of speech. Help me to continue to speak the truth in love, no matter the consequences.

DAY 33 ★ THE FREEDOM OF SPEECH

Opponents must be gently instructed, in the
hope that God will grant them repentance
leading them to a knowledge of the truth.
—2 TIMOTHY 2:25

Paul understood the plight of men, that they were filled by the evil one and needed saving. He also knew that folks couldn't respond to the gospel if they didn't hear it first. As he wrote in his letter to the Romans,

> How, then, can [sinners] call on the one they have not believed in? And how can they believe in the one of whom they have not heard? And how can they hear without someone preaching to them? (10:14)

Paul knew that the common citizens, the jailers, the rulers of the day—everyone—needed to *hear* the word of truth if they were going to move on it. And so even in prison Paul exercised his God-given freedom to speak, a freedom that couldn't be taken away by anyone.

Even before he was imprisoned Paul knew that preaching the truth would have consequences. He knew he'd be mocked, belittled, beaten, and stoned. Still, he went to the Gentiles and preached the message of the cross. Why? As he wrote,

> The message of the cross is foolishness to those who are perishing, but to us who are being saved it is the power of God. For it is written:
>
> > "I will destroy the wisdom of the wise;
> > the intelligence of the intelligent I will frustrate."
> > (1 Cor. 1:18–19)

Paul knew the world would find the story of Jesus to be insane. Born of a virgin? Lived a sinless life? Crucified for our sin? Conquered death on our behalf? Ascended to heaven and is seated at the right hand of the Father? How could a faithless world find that to be anything but foolish? Yet Paul knew it was the kind of foolishness that could save anyone who believed in it.

Children of the Almighty and citizens of America, don't miss this: we have an obligation to warn those who are dead in their sins, controlled by the evil one and his minions (Eph. 2:2). And we need to speak this truth in love, in kindness, instructing them in the hopes that God will bring them to repentance (2 Tim. 2:25). God told us to speak out—it's our God-given responsibility—so that we might bring freedom to those enslaved to sin.

As for me, I plan to exercise my obligation to speech because I believe the truths of the Bible can save my neighbors from death and my country from chaos. So even if the masses think it's foolishness, even if the government enacts laws to shut me up, I'm gonna keep on preaching. And if the day comes when they tell me I can't call a sin a sin, or I can't spread the good news of Jesus, or I can't talk about how America should return to the truths of the Almighty, guess who they can throw in a jail cell, just like Paul? Me. Why? Because no government will take away my God-given and Founding-Father-recognized right to speak the truth that might save their very souls.

If Jesus is the only hope for America—and I believe he is—that hope hangs on the Christian's exercise of his or her freedom of speech. Without it, how can we speak truth to the lie?

★　　★　　★

Lord, thank you for giving us your Word, which shows us the way to eternal life. Help me to fulfill my responsibility to speak the truth so that I might bring freedom to those who are enslaved to sin.

DAY 34 ★ USING FREEDOM TO SPEAK TRUTH

Have I now become your enemy by telling you the truth?
—GALATIANS 4:16

As I mentioned in Day 15, I agreed to an interview in 2013 with a men's magazine that caused a lot of ruckus. I'd exercised my freedom to speak the truth of God's Word, and those under the influence of the evil one exercised their free speech to influence the television network to suspend me from *Duck Dynasty*. Many who watched the show, people of faith, used their rights of speech and influenced the network to reinstate me.

Speech, speech, speech—we'd all used it for different purposes. And sure, the government didn't keep me from speaking or prosecute me under some hate-speech legislation—an act I think would be in violation of the Constitution—but some suggested they should. Some suggested that creating new legislation might be a way to shut up folks like me in the future.

Enact a law prohibiting me from speaking what the Bible says?

Here in America?

Huh?

In the end everything was sorted out in my favor, and I'm grateful for that. But is it hard to imagine a day when the masses, their nonprofits, the worldly corporations, and a corrupt government will work together to shut down the spread of the gospel message? Hardly. There's no better way for a faithless world to insulate itself from conviction and pursue their own desires than to shut down the Christian's right of speech. Just look at Russia, China, and so many of the Muslim-controlled countries. See how quickly tyranny can spread when the evil one persuades us with his lies, primarily the lie that Christians shouldn't have the right to speak the truth?

The Bible teaches me to love my neighbor as much as I love myself, and I love myself enough to try and avoid the eternal punishment for all my sins. So if I'm to love my neighbor just as much, shouldn't I do whatever I can to warn my brothers of the coming punishment for their sin? Shouldn't I exercise my freedom of speech to that end?

No doubt.

It's not hate speech to give someone the truth that will save their souls. It's love speech. And so no amount of public ridicule from faithless people, no godless group, and no number of high-minded professors can keep me from sharing the truth in love. A magazine article poking fun at me won't keep me from sharing the truth in love. Losing sponsors or sales or money won't stop me from sharing the truth in love. And if the government enacts tyrannical laws that keep me from sharing my faith, that won't keep me from speaking the truth in love either. Why? I have an obligation to share the truth that sets men free.

Regardless of the consequences.

Regardless of whether the world thinks it's foolishness.

After all, it's that foolishness that might save their souls.

Interview after interview, time after time, the media has attacked my love for Jesus and my commitment to his truth. As we say down here in Louisiana, it don't bother me a lick. Jesus used his freedom to preach the truth all the way to the cross. Paul used his freedom of speech to preach the good news even when it landed him in prison and cost him his life. God's people are his prophetic voice in America, and it's time to use our freedom to preach the good news. If we do, we can turn this ship around before we lose our right to speak.

★   ★   ★

Lord, thank you for the truth that sets men free. May Christians all over America—including me—continue to preach the gospel and speak the truth in love, regardless of the consequences.

DAY 35 ★ RELIGIOUS LIBERTY

In the same way, let your light shine before others, that they may see your good deeds and glorify your Father in heaven.
—MATTHEW 5:16

We've entered a new era in American history. Once, we were a country founded on Christian principles. Then our Christian principles came under attack as a government of godless men removed the statues, signs, and symbols of our country's biblical heritage from the public square. Now, our very right to express our personal faith in schools, politics, and even our own businesses is under attack.

Consider how our politicians have disregarded the Founding Fathers' wisdom and wishes. They've done their level best to remove God from our public schools. In the early 1960s, the Supreme Court ruled that teachers and principals couldn't lead prayers. Christian symbols were systematically removed from schools too. Even today those symbols continue to be removed.[1]

Likewise, politicians, courts, and citizens alike have targeted Christian symbols on public land. For instance, the Supreme Court declared that certain state courthouses cannot publicly display the Ten Commandments, even though a depiction of Moses carrying the commandments is displayed on the frieze of the Supreme Court building.

State governments are cracking down on the private exercise of religious beliefs too. In 2012, Jack Phillips, a Colorado baker, refused to bake a cake for a same-sex couple. Why? He's a Christian who believes that biblical marriage is between a man and a woman. What's more, he had the audacity to allow his Christian beliefs to influence his business practices.

What was the result of Phillips standing by his convictions? The couple filed a complaint with the Colorado Civil Rights Commission and prevailed: "Colorado has barred Phillips from making any more wedding cakes because he refuses to abide by its civil rights laws."[2]

A private baker, who runs a private business, cannot exercise his religion through that business? I suppose it's fair to say that Colorado's antidiscrimination legislation allowed discrimination against Christian faith.

Up until the American Revolution, liberty—particularly religious liberty—was an ideal at best. But our Founding Fathers knew true and lasting liberty could only be established when the people of this country recognized that all were created equal and that they were endowed by the Almighty with certain inalienable rights. The foundational right, the one embodied in the First Amendment, was the right to practice one's Christian faith.

Didn't the Founding Fathers know best?

We are living in an age when governments are removing expressions of faith left and right. Government actors are trying to shut down the practice of our faith in the public square, where an increasing tyranny of godlessness seeks to silence us. Are you okay with this? I'm not.

American Christian: *It's time to take some responsibility.*

The organizers of the American Revolution were godly men who wanted *you* to have the freedom to practice your Christian beliefs. They wanted you to exercise your faith in your public and private life. They wanted you to speak out about it and to assemble in your church. And they wanted you to build your life and the life of this country on the only sure foundation: the foundation of King Jesus' Word.

* * *

Jesus, your Word is the only sure foundation for my life and the life of our nation. Show me how I can take responsibility to exercise my faith in the public square and make sure others have the freedom to do so too.

DAY 36 ★ THE FREEDOM TO BEAR ARMS

When a strong man, fully armed, guards his own house, his possessions are safe.
—LUKE 11:21

ards on the table: I'm a gun-toting, NRA card–carrying, Second Amendment supporter. And chances are, if you're reading this book, you already knew that. I host a podcast that's fielded sponsorship requests from companies like iTarget (a home firearm training system), TacPack (a tactical gear retailer), and My Patriot Supply (a company some might call a prepper warehouse). So I suppose some might call me biased. After all, I'm an old-timey patriot who takes self-sufficiency seriously.

Our Founding Fathers took self-sufficiency seriously too. They knew a day might come when We the People might need to defend ourselves against a tyrannical form of government that wanted nothing more than to take away our liberties, especially our religious liberties. And even though men such as George Washington, James Madison, and John Adams surely knew violent men might use guns to murder others, they made no attempt to prohibit the people from owning guns. In fact, they made gun ownership a fundamental right by way of the Second Amendment to our Constitution, which stipulates, "A well regulated Militia, being necessary to the security of a free State, the right of the people to keep and bear arms, shall not be infringed."[1]

The Second Amendment wasn't drafted to protect our right to hunt. It wasn't simply a provision to allow us to protect our homes from intruders. It certainly wasn't drafted to protect our right to let a few rounds loose at a gun range either. It was a provision passed by the Founding Fathers who knew that firearms might be necessary one day to deter future fascists.

Don't believe me? Consider what the Founders said themselves.

In a letter to Alexander Hamilton, George Washington wrote:

It may be laid down as a primary position, and the basis of our system, that every Citizen who enjoys the protection of a free Government, owes not only a proportion of his property, but even his personal services to the defence of it, and consequently that the Citizens of America (with a few legal and official exceptions) from 18 to 50 Years of Age should be borne on the Militia Rolls, provided with uniform Arms, and so far accustomed to the use of them, that the Total strength of the Country might be called forth at a Short Notice on any very interesting Emergency.[2]

Similarly, Thomas Jefferson penned the following in a letter to William Stephens Smith (the son-in-law of John Adams): "What country can preserve [its] liberties if their rulers are not warned from time to time that their people preserve the spirit of resistance? Let them take arms."[3]

The right to bear arms was a nonnegotiable for our Founding Fathers. It was so important that it was the constitutional amendment that immediately followed the First Amendment, which guaranteed free speech, freedom of religion, and freedom of assembly. And this right to bear arms was held in high esteem for more than two hundred years.

★　　★　　★

God, thank you for the freedom our Constitution gives us to defend our families and loved ones. May I respect this fundamental right to preserve our liberties.

DAY 37 ★ JESUS IN TODAY'S POLITICS

Your kingdom come,
your will be done,
    on earth as it is in heaven.
—MATTHEW 6:10

These days, it's mighty hard to find the King in our political parties, and that goes for both Republicans and Democrats. Our news cycle is dominated by partisan bickering. Both sides spin up millions of dollars through campaign contributions and gin up as much dirt as they can on the opposition. Both sides claim only they can sort out the problems that plague our country. It's a cycle that continues election after election. But look around. Are things getting any better?

We're more divided than ever. We're so divided, in fact, that we choose our news outlets based on whether we're right-wingers or left-wingers.

We're more violent than ever, a country that routinely experiences mass shootings at the hands of demonically influenced lunatics.

We're more immoral than ever, a country entertained by programming that contains illicit sex. (Which is to say nothing of the filth on the internet.)

The family is in decline.

Babies are being aborted.

There are riots in the streets.

What was once called evil is now called good.

And if all of this isn't bad enough, so many of our politicians, the folks who are supposed to be "for the people," fall prey to corruption. Though they're supposed to represent the people, they make a fortune from the business of politics.

What's the problem?

Listen up, America.

There's a vast difference between the Supreme Court and the Supreme Being. The King's laws for living supersede the laws of any man-made rules and regulations. What's more, the King's laws have eternity riding on them. But the sad truth is, though we were once a country who did their best to follow the King, we've traded God's laws for laws fashioned in the shape of our own desires. "We the People" have cast our votes for the politics of self-indulgence, self-interest, and self-gratification. We've voted for the very things that steal our freedoms, kill our society, and destroy our country. And we did all these things without checking in with King Jesus first.

Yes, in our delusion, we've decided we're capable of governing ourselves without reference to the policies of King Jesus, policies established in love. And man-made laws based on our finite judgment have only ever led us astray. There's good news, though. As followers of Christ, we've been given the antidote to America's soul sickness. What's the antidote? Jesus Politics.

Jesus—God with Us—came in the midst of an ancient political quagmire. He made his home with the Jewish people, a people who were under the left thumb of godless political rulers (the Romans) and the right thumb of God-forgetting religious leaders. In that broken political system, he announced the truth. He was the King, and aligning ourselves with his ways would lead to peace, prosperity, and a full life, even in the middle of so much brokenness. That's not all, though. Jesus also tasked us to pray that his kingdom would come on earth as it is in heaven. And in addition to praying, he asked us to bring the kingdom into the world around us through every means possible, including, if possible, political means.

★　　★　　★

King Jesus, thank you for coming to earth and showing us the way that leads to peace, prosperity, and a full life. May your kingdom come and your will be done on earth as it is in heaven.

DAY 38 ★ AMERICA'S SPIRITUAL PROBLEM

For although they knew God, they neither glorified him as God nor gave thanks to him, but their thinking became futile and their foolish hearts were darkened.
—ROMANS 1:21

The problem with our country isn't a problem that can be solved by any particular political party. After all, America's problem isn't a flesh-and-blood problem; it's a powers-and-principalities problem.

The evil one is working overtime to convince America that God is dead or, at the least, God is unnecessary. The evil one's convinced us that our freedoms weren't founded in God, but rather they were granted to allow us to chase our every desire. The evil one twisted those desires and used them to influence the way we vote. As a result, the Enemy has sneaked into America through politicians who reflect the character of its people. And what is that character? The apostle Paul put it this way:

> For although they knew God, they neither glorified him as God nor gave thanks to him, but their thinking became futile and their foolish hearts were darkened. Although they claimed to be wise, they became fools and exchanged the glory of the immortal God for images made to look like a mortal human being and birds and animals and reptiles.
>
> Therefore God gave them over in the sinful desires of their hearts to sexual impurity for the degrading of their bodies with one another. They exchanged the truth about God for a lie, and worshiped and served created things rather than the Creator—who is forever praised. (Rom. 1:21–25)

83

What are the characteristics of those who follow the evil one? They are a people who don't worship God. A people whose hearts are foolish and darkened. A people who worship the animals, the environment, maybe even the climate. A people who are sexually immoral, who serve every lust. Sound familiar?

Yes, we're certainly locked in a battle for the soul of America. If we're going to win that battle, though, we need a spiritual solution, not one born from the hearts of men. And as people of the King, as citizens of the kingdom of heaven, we need a strategy for bringing that spiritual solution "on earth as it is in heaven." We need a common strategy, a statement of purpose. What do we need? We need a kingdom manifesto.

Karl Marx and his commie buddies corrupted the word *manifesto* with his *Communist Manifesto*. But what if we reclaimed and redeemed the word? After all, a manifesto is no more than a declaration of intent, whether for good or bad. It's a decisive, provocative statement of action. Manifestos typically aren't politically correct. They don't coddle those who disagree. Maybe we Christians, the citizens of the kingdom of heaven on earth, need our own manifesto. Maybe we need a unifying call to action for all citizens of the kingdom of heaven on earth.

God, the evil one is working overtime in America to deceive so many people. May I unite with my brothers and sisters in Christ to take action and proclaim the truth of your kingdom.

DAY 39 ★ A KINGDOM FOUNDATION

Everyone who hears these words of mine and puts them into practice is like a wise man who built his house on the rock.
—MATTHEW 7:24

The United States of America was built on a godly foundation, a kingdom foundation.

In October 1829, Noah Webster wrote a letter to James Madison that recounted their history together, how they met in 1782, when Webster visited Philadelphia (the seat of the young US government at the time) to share the early drafts of a small book. That book eventually grew into a two-volume dictionary, the one we all know and love today. But Webster wasn't writing to discuss his dictionary. So once he'd dispensed with the pleasantries, he launched into his thoughts on a far more important matter: the drafting of a new constitution for the Commonwealth of Virginia.

In his letter, Webster offered his well-reasoned opinion about the role of the Almighty in government:

> I sincerely hope that Virginia, in her new Constitution, will avow some fundamental errors, in the principle of representation, which, in my opinion, have marred the constitutions of other States, & may yet shorten the duration of our republican form of government. I know not whether I am singular in the opinion; but it is my decided opinion, that the christian religion, in its purity, is the basis or rather the source of all genuine freedom in government. I speak not of the religion which gives the property & power of a state to [maritus] & dignitaries. I speak of the religion which was preached by Christ & his apostles, which breathes love to God & love to man. And I am persuaded that no civil government of a republican

form can exist & be durable, in which the principles of that religion have not a controlling influence.[1]

Webster was a man of opinion and conviction. And it was his opinion and conviction that Virginia—and by extension, all of America—needed an unshakable, immovable, bedrock foundation. That foundation was Christianity.

Webster wasn't alone, of course. Many (if not all) of the Founding Fathers considered the Bible as the foundation and framing of our country. And though I'll not retread all that ground here, I'll recap a little. Consider George Washington, a devout Christian, who knew virtue and morality couldn't exist without the influence of God. In his 1796 farewell address, Washington said, "Whatever may be conceded to the influence of refined education on minds of peculiar structure—reason & experience both forbid us to expect that National morality can prevail in exclusion of religious principle."[2] In addition, Washington said, "To the distinguished Character of Patriot, it should be our highest Glory to add the more distinguished Character of Christian."[3]

★   ★   ★

Lord, thank you for the Founding Fathers, who built America on the bedrock foundation of Christianity. May we honor their legacy by being faithful to you and upholding biblical truth.

DAY 40 ★ THE KINGDOM THAT ENDURES

All people are like grass,
    and all their glory is like the flowers of the field;
the grass withers and the flowers fall,
    but the word of the Lord endures forever.
—1 PETER 1:24–25

John Adams, the second president of the United States, affirmed that America was built on a foundation of Christianity:

> The general principles, on which the Fathers achieved independence, were the only Principles in which that beautiful Assembly of young Gentlemen could Unite. . . . And what were these general Principles? I answer, the general Principles of Christianity, in which all these Sects were United.[1]

In fact, Adams also believed a system of laws based on God's Word would lead to a virtuous utopia, a veritable paradise.[2]

Patrick Henry, a devout Christian, stated, "The great pillars of all government and of social life . . . [are] virtue, morality, and religion. This is the armor, my friend, and this alone, that renders us invincible."[3]

The Founding Fathers knew the Scriptures, and they would have understood the teachings of Jesus in the gospel of Matthew. In the Sermon on the Mount, he preached about good deeds, hate, adultery, and divorce. He taught us to love our enemies and to give to the needy. He taught us to pray, fast, and store up treasures in the hereafter. And as he concluded his sermon, he ended with a simple teaching:

> Therefore, everyone who hears these words of mine and puts them into practice is like a wise man who built his house on the rock. The rain came down, the streams rose, and the winds blew and

beat against that house; yet it did not fall, because it had its foundation on the rock. But everyone who hears these words of mine and does not put them into practice is like a foolish man who built his house on sand. The rain came down, the streams rose, and the winds blew and beat against that house, and it fell with a great crash. (Matt. 7:24–28)

It's safe to assume the godly men who founded our great republic knew the trouble that comes when a country is built on the flimsy philosophies of men. After all, they'd experienced firsthand the issues that came with a self-serving, man-centered, truth-denying, tyrannical monarchy. So they came together under the belief that a biblical foundation would create something different. Something just and peaceful and loving. Something kingdom centered. Something as enduring as the Scriptures themselves. After all, to paraphrase the Scriptures: "All governments are like grass, and their glory is like the flowers of the field; the grass withers and the flowers fall, but the word of the Lord endures forever" (1 Peter 1:24–25).

Jesus, all the flimsy philosophies of this world are only temporary. Help me to build my life and my family on the enduring, solid rock of your Word.

★ *PART III* ★

HEALING

GRACIOUS WORDS ARE A HONEYCOMB, SWEET TO THE SOUL AND HEALING TO THE BONES.

—PROVERBS 16:24

DAY 41 ★ THE GRACE OF GOD

By the grace of God I am what I am, and his
grace to me was not without effect.
—1 CORINTHIANS 15:10

In the first month of my conversion, one of my old buddies came along and asked me to go fishing with him. Fishing with an old friend in the middle of the afternoon couldn't hurt anything, could it? I asked him whether there was water in his cooler, and he said there was. With that, we were off.

An hour into our fishing expedition, with the Louisiana sun beating down on our boat, I went for the water. To my surprise, I discovered that he'd only brought a couple of six packs of beer. (Should I have been surprised? Liars lie, after all.) It was midday, and humidity had sucked every ounce of moisture from me. What was a thirsty man supposed to do? Couldn't I drink a beer or two and be fine? So I grabbed a can, pulled the tab, and drank.

Then I pulled the tab on another can.

Then another.

A few hours, a mess of catfish, and too many beers later, we headed back. When I stumbled back into the trailer, there was Miss Kay, sitting in her rocker and chatting with my parents who'd come for an unexpected visit. She knew in an instant, but she asked anyway.

"Have you been drinking again?"

"It was all he had," I said, half-lit as I stumbled to the bedroom.

I don't remember the crash landing, but I remember waking up hungover. It was Sunday, and when it came time to get ready for church, I told Miss Kay I didn't feel well. I'd rather stay home, I told her, and she capitulated at first. My mother, though, was not having a lick of it. She marched into my room, stared me down, and said, "Phil, get up. You're going to church."

That settled that.

I sat through that church service, ashamed that I'd been tricked into drinking. I don't remember the sermon. I don't remember the songs we sang. I do remember the sense of conviction that plagued me throughout the service. I knew the truth—the truth that had set me free—and yet I'd fallen into the schemes of an untrustworthy friend. I'd fallen for the lie.

Near the end of the service, the preacher, Bill Smith, stood and offered an invitation to repent and turn to Jesus, and before the first bar of the first song was sung, I started making my way to the front. Bill met me there, and I told him I'd managed to get commode-hugging drunk the day before. He received my confession with more grace than I deserved, and after the invitation song was sung, he stood and shared my struggle with the congregation.

To my great amazement, no one heaped judgment or shame on me. In fact, there was nothing but acceptance and love. An elderly lady, one I'd never met, came to me and said, "I love you, and I'm proud of you." Another approached me and said, "God forgives you. That's what the grace of God is all about. Get up and keep walking."

God, thank you for your forgiveness and your amazing grace. May I be faithful to follow you—and when I stumble and fall, may I get up and keep walking, knowing that your grace covers all my sins.

DAY 42 ★ LOVE YOUR NEIGHBORS

"Love the Lord your God with all your heart and with all your soul and with all your strength and with all your mind"; and, "Love your neighbor as yourself."
—LUKE 10:27

Jesus came preaching the unifying love of God. But he didn't just preach it. He embodied it. He spent time with men and women, rich and poor, sick and healthy, Jews and Gentiles. He asked a Roman employee—Matthew, the tax collector—to become his disciple. He also asked a Jewish zealot who would have hated that Roman tax collector—Peter—to follow along. He touched the lepers (Matt. 8:2–3). He spent time with the hated Samaritans, including a second-class, outcast, divorced-five-times-over Samaritan woman (John 4:1–42). Jesus came, and he showed no favoritism, only love for all.

To remove any doubt about the law of impartial love, Jesus made himself clear. In the book of Luke, a lawyer asked Jesus how he might inherit eternal life. Jesus flipped the question around and asked what the Scriptures had to say on the matter. The lawyer responded by quoting the law, and said, "'Love the Lord your God with all your heart and with all your soul and with all your strength and with all your mind'; and 'Love your neighbor as yourself'" (10:27). After Jesus agreed with his answer, the lawyer asked, "And who is my neighbor?" (v. 29).

Lawyers—always splitting hairs.

The question led Jesus to his clearest teaching on equality and unity, and he did it all through a parable. You may recall it. A Jewish man was on his way to Jerusalem when he was attacked by robbers, Jesus said. Left on the road for dead, the man was in dire need of help. A Jewish priest happened past him on the road, but he didn't stop to help. Instead, he crossed to the other side of the road. A Levite—another devoted Jewish man—likewise refused to help him and crossed to the other side of the road. But then a Samaritan, a man despised by the Jews, passed by and helped the beaten and bloody man. He bandaged his wounds and gave him a drink. He then took him to a local inn and left money for the owner so that the man would be taken care of.

Jesus finished the parable and then asked the lawyer, "Which of these three do you think was a neighbor to the man who fell into the hands of the robbers?"

"The one who had mercy on him," he said of the Samaritan.

"Go and do likewise," Jesus said (vv. 30–37).

Jesus' teaching through this parable was simple. All people are our neighbors, even those of different nationalities or ethnicities. Even those of different political beliefs, just like the Jew and Samaritan. Even those whom we might consider our enemies. And how are we to treat those neighbors, those we see as different? We're to treat them just as we would want to be treated—with self-sacrificing love.

★　★　★

God, it's not easy to love my neighbors, especially those I see as different. Give me your compassion and perspective so that I can treat even my enemies with your love.

DAY 43 ★ A DEMONIC DELIVERANCE

Our struggle is not against flesh and blood, but against the rulers, against the authorities, against the powers of this dark world and against the spiritual forces of evil in the heavenly realms.
—EPHESIANS 6:12

Years ago I visited a rehab facility, and a patient went on a tirade. She told me my religion and politics weren't welcome in the place. She hollered and yelled and cussed at me. Then she stormed out of the room.

The receptionist stopped by to make sure I wasn't bothered. I told her I wasn't and asked whether I could sit with this patient for a while. The receptionist said, "Sure, but good luck."

We waited in the lobby, and the patient returned, cursing up a storm. When she was finished, I said, "I can't help you if you don't listen." I reckon I struck the right tone, because she calmed a little and asked, "What'dya got?"

I gave the woman the good news of Jesus and showed how she'd come under the influence of the evil one. Hatred, malice, name-calling, cursing—these were all tools of the evil one to separate us from the saving message of Jesus, I told her, but there was good news. Right then, the woman slammed her head on the table and made a low gurgle like something was stuck in her throat. She vomited and then ran to the bathroom. After a few minutes she came out, cleaned-up and quieter.

"Can y'all help me?" she begged.

"Jesus can help anyone who calls on his name," I said.

I shared the good news of Jesus, how he'd come to free us from the enemy's grip. I told her that all her sins could be forgiven and that she could have eternal life. She didn't have to see me as her enemy, I said, and she could join my family, the family of God. She listened, then asked if I might come back the next day. I agreed.

When I showed up the next day, she was clean-faced and smiling. She asked me to baptize her in the river that ran past the facility. I raised her from the waters, and the woman who'd hated me the day before was now my sister in Christ.

The receptionist told me she thought it was nothing short of a miracle. It was a demonic deliverance, she said. Looking back on it, I suppose she was right. The enemy of the Almighty thought anger, hatred, name-calling, and cursing could drive me away from that girl who needed nothing more than Jesus. But the lies of the enemy are no match for the unifying truth of God.

The good news of the gospel is that it frees us from the lies (and possession) of the enemy. It can bring ultimate unity, if only we believe it. The gospel brings together folks of every ethnicity, nationality, economic class, and gender. It heals the division in our country.

American church, our country is more divided than ever. But we have the greatest tool for freeing the world of the lie. We have the Word of Truth. It's the tool that might make a family of us again. So let's get back to it. When we gather on Sunday mornings, let's model a love for our neighbors that shows no favoritism based on class, color, or nationality. Let's carry the truth of Christ's unity out into the workplace, into public schools, into the rehab centers. Let's share it with those who are possessed by their father, the evil one, and let's watch deliverance happen.

★   ★   ★

God, your truth can unify people of all classes, colors, and nationalities. May we carry the Word of Truth everywhere we go, ready to share it with those who need deliverance from the evil one.

DAY 44 ★ REDNECKS HELPING REDNECKS

Do not forget to do good and to share with others,
for with such sacrifices God is pleased.
—HEBREWS 13:16

For years, old Jimmy Red was on the welfare roll. Why? Raised poor, not a whole lot of education, and little opportunity or access to money, it was difficult for him to find long-term work. He took jobs from time to time, but nothing ever stuck. So he used the government to fill the gaps.

I knew Jimmy, though. I knew, with a little opportunity and access to resources, he'd work hard and do just fine. So I hatched a plan. I bought a truck, one that Red could use.

Months after I bought that truck, I stood on an old rutted road near my homeplace. A film crew had come to talk about my thoughts on welfare, so I decided to take them on a field trip. I wanted them to see what happens when one redneck offers another redneck a leg up. I wanted to show them how to eliminate the welfare state in America.

We made our way to a place where Jimmy Red was in his truck, hard at work under the afternoon sun. He was busy smoothing out the potholes created by heavy traffic. I told the film crew how I'd bought that old eighteen-wheel hauling rig that Jimmy used to move stone, gravel, dirt, whatever. I held the title to the truck, but I'd told Red, if he'd get his commercial driver's license, he could use the truck for construction jobs and keep whatever he made off the hauls. He had to pay for his own gas and insurance. And any permitting too. But I promised Jimmy I wouldn't take a red cent of his profit.

When Jimmy turned off the rig and stepped out of the cab, I called him over to the patch of road where I was with the film crew.

In a camouflage LSU hat and sleeveless T-shirt, he smiled for the camera.

I shared how Red had become a hard worker, the type of man who'd become quite industrious since he jumped off the welfare roll. He moved dirt, hauled stone, did a little excavation work, I said. But that wasn't all. With the money he made from his hauls, he'd begun reclaiming junk for resale, stuff his wife called *antiques*. He bought it for pennies and sold it for dollars. Jimmy Red, I said, had become an entrepreneur. A certifiable capitalist.

I pointed to the patch of ground Red had smoothed over so it was passable.

Jimmy kicked at the dirt, but I knew he was proud of his work. He'd done something of value, and he'd earned a day's wage as a result.

A few years ago, Red didn't have a job or a means to provide food. He'd once been comfortable taking the taxpayers' money, but now, he'd been given an opportunity to earn his wages through hard work. He'd more than made good on it. And how had he gotten that opportunity? Through Robertson-care, my personal program to end local poverty, which comes with only one condition: use what you've been given to earn a living.

Old Jimmy Red has been hauling for me for some time now. He has plenty to eat, his family has what they need, and he's not dependent on the government to get ahead. Why? Because one redneck used his capital to help out another redneck.

Lord, you have created each of us to honor you in our work and provide for our families. Thank you for giving me what I need, and show me how I can share it to help others.

DAY 45 ★ SOLVING THE MURDER PROBLEM

You have heard that it was said to the people long ago,
"You shall not murder, and anyone who murders will be
subject to judgment." But I tell you anyone who is angry
with a brother or sister will be subject to judgment.
—MATTHEW 5:21–22

Murder has been in the human heart since the beginning. In fact, the third human being on the planet murdered the fourth. Remember the story?

Cain worked the soil. Abel kept flocks. Both made offerings to the Lord. But all offerings are not created equally. "The Lord looked with favor on Abel and his offering, but on Cain and his offering he did not look with favor" (Gen. 4:4–5). Cain discovered the Almighty favored Abel's offering, and Cain did not take the news well. The Bible records that Cain became angry and "his face was downcast" (v. 5).

God reminded Cain that blessing would come if he'd commit himself to doing right. Then the Almighty warned, "If you do not do what is right, sin is crouching at your door; it desires to have you, but you must rule over it" (v. 7). But Cain turned his back on God's instruction. Cain invited his brother into the field, and there he dispatched him in cold blood.

The instrument of murder used by Cain is never mentioned. Was it a rock? A club? A knife? The Bible doesn't say. To be plainer, it doesn't really matter. After all, the instrument of murder matters less than the motive underlying it. And what was that motive? Hate inspired by the evil one.

John, the beloved follower of King Jesus, said as much. In a letter to the early church, he wrote of the origins of murder and the antidote for it:

For this is the message you heard from the beginning: We should love one another. Do not be like Cain, who belonged to the evil one and murdered his brother. And why did he murder him? Because his own actions were evil and his brother's were righteous. (1 John 3:11–12)

See the problem? It ain't the guns or the knives or the sticks or the stones. It's not even the violent movies or video games. Murder comes from a condition of the heart that is influenced by the evil one. But if a man gives himself to the love of the King, his hate-filled, murderous heart will be replaced with a heart full of the King's love.

King Jesus knew the truth about murder, and he cautioned his followers to root out all demonically inspired anger. He taught, "You have heard that it was said to the people long ago, 'You shall not murder, and anyone who murders will be subject to judgment.' But I tell you that anyone who is angry with a brother or sister will be subject to judgment" (Matt. 5:21–22).

There's that word again: *anger*.

The murder problem that's plaguing America (the one that's been plaguing humanity since forever) isn't a gun problem; it's an anger problem, a hate problem, a lack-of-love problem. It's a spiritual health problem. And so long as we're mired in anger, hate, and malice, we'll have chaos in our schools and in our streets. We'll have continuing murder, whether by AR-15s, shotguns, knives, clubs, rocks, or ropes.

Yes, there's only one solution for the current murder problem in America. We have to return to the principles of the King. Where he reigns, murder has no place. Where his love is celebrated, death meets its demise. Put another way, when the love rate is high, the murder rate is low.

★   ★   ★

Lord, for those who struggle with anger, I pray that you would intervene. Show me how I can spread your love to overcome the hate and anger that can lead to murder today.

DAY 46 ★ HEALING THE GUN-VIOLENCE CRISIS

Love does no harm to a neighbor. Therefore love is the fulfillment of the law.
—ROMANS 13:10

It is my firm, well-studied, river-rat reasoned opinion that removing firearms from the hands of the people will not remove hate from their hearts. What's more, removing those firearms might lead to a creeping tyranny, to a government whose power is no longer restrained by the power of its own people. So it's my estimation that advancing gun-control measures is creating a problem we've never had (tyranny) without solving a problem we've always had (murder in our hearts).

According to a Pew Research poll, 30 percent of Americans own a gun and 11 percent live in a gun-owning home.[1] That means there are roughly ninety-eight million gun owners in America. And of those ninety-eight million gun owners, how many have committed a mass shooting in 2018? Less than one thousandth of 1 percent. I know hundreds of gun owners, and I've spoken to thousands over the years. Many of them are Christian men and women, and though they're well-armed, it's never crossed their minds to walk into a school and shoot up the joint. They've never considered using a firearm for illegal purposes. And most never would. Why? Because as citizens of the kingdom, those gun owners are ruled by the law of love.

The solution for America's gun-violence crisis is to return to the King's law, the law of love. But how do we do that? Consider the following steps:

- Instead of promoting new gun legislation, promote the love of the King; preach it to the world around you.

- Vote for politicians who advance the King's love, too, knowing that's the only solution for America's murder problem.
- Promote policies that protect the Founding Fathers' wisdom that saw gun ownership as a right and a way to defend our freedoms (as well as our neighbors) from a government opposed to the King.
- Hold the line on the law of love, and if enough of us do, we might see a country that remains free enough to experience the love that casts out all fear, anger, hate, and malice (Eph. 4:31).

Don't be persuaded by the godless politicians and mainstream media who believe they can bring gun violence to an end without addressing the heart of the matter. Don't fall for their promises of peace and prosperity without a return to the King. Don't place your trust in political solutions. Place your trust in Jesus Politics and in the heart change only he can bring. Promote politicians who understand Jesus Politics, who know the solution to America's murder problem lies in the human heart and who promote spiritual solutions. Vote in line with the Founding Fathers and the King. And as you use your vote and your voice accordingly, realize you're protecting this country from a future of creeping godless tyranny.

★   ★   ★

King Jesus, as a citizen of your kingdom, help me to live by the law of love. Help me to love my neighbors and use my voice to promote spiritual solutions to America's gun-violence crisis.

DAY 47 ★ WORSHIP THE CREATOR, NOT CREATION

**They exchanged the truth about God for a lie,
and worshiped and served created things rather
than the Creator—who is forever praised.**
—ROMANS 1:25

All of creation is meant to point us to the King, to teach us about the King, and to spread the news of his kingdom. This much is true. But from the beginning, lawless people have elevated the creation over the Creator. They've worshipped Mother Nature instead of Father God.

Don't believe me? Paul said as much: "Although [mankind] claimed to be wise, they became fools and exchanged the glory of the immortal God for images made to look like a mortal human being and birds and animals and reptiles" (Rom. 1:22–23). What was the result of this exchange?

> Therefore God gave them over in the sinful desires of their hearts to sexual impurity for the degrading of their bodies with one another. They exchanged the truth about God for a lie, and worshiped and served created things rather than the Creator—who is forever praised. (vv. 24–25)

See there? When we worship the creation over the Creator, we're wading into troubled waters.

And listen up, millennial environmentalists, worship of the creation is a dead end. Why? Because if you think climate change is bad, just wait till the judgment of the King comes. The apostle Peter, the one who'd been given the keys to the kingdom, described that event:

> But the day of the Lord will come like a thief. The heavens will disappear with a roar; the elements will be destroyed by fire, and the earth and everything done in it will be laid bare. (2 Peter 3:10)

The elements will be destroyed by fire. See there, global warming is a biblical guarantee. But if you worship the King, if you honor him above the environment, you'll experience something even better than what we have here, namely, a new and perfect earth with the city of God at its center. What will that city look like? In the book of Revelation, John shared:

> Then I saw "a new heaven and a new earth," for the first heaven and the first earth had passed away, and there was no longer any sea. I saw the Holy City, the new Jerusalem, coming down out of heaven from God, prepared as a bride beautifully dressed for her husband. And I heard a loud voice from the throne saying, "Look! God's dwelling place is now among the people, and he will dwell with them. They will be his people, and God himself will be with them and be their God. 'He will wipe every tear from their eyes. There will be no more death' or mourning or crying or pain, for the old order of things has passed away."
>
> He who was seated on the throne said, "I am making everything new!" (21:1–5)

Imagine the new earth and the city of God in it: crystal-clear water, a tree of life bearing not one but twelve crops worth of fruit, no death, no night, a place where kingdom citizens reign forever and ever with the King (Rev. 22:1–5). Doesn't that sound so much better than the world we're trying to save? It does to me.

★　　★　　★

God, I praise you for your beautiful creation, which displays your majesty and love for us. While this earth and everything in it are passing away, I look forward to spending eternity in the new earth, where you are making all things new!

DAY 48 ★ BIBLICAL ENVIRONMENTALISM

How many are your works, LORD!
   In wisdom you made them all;
   the earth is full of your creatures.
—PSALM 104:24

The environment is God's gift to us, river rats and city slickers alike. So no matter where you make your home, pay attention to the sunrise that takes your breath away. Consider the roar of the ocean on your family vacation or take in the beauty of your nearest national park. Recall how awe-inspiring it is to see a muskrat, a deer, or a flock of mallards in the wild. The call of creation is a call to worship the Almighty if we'll let it be. But if we worship the creation instead of the Creator, our end will be no different than the end of nature itself: total destruction.

Now listen, I'm not saying green energy is bad. I'm not knocking solar power or electric cars or windmills. You want to drive around in an electric go-cart a full-grown man can't fit into? Go for it, dude. I'll support you. What I am saying, though, is to have a little common sense. Don't be bamboozled by the Chicken Little politicians who claim the sky is falling, who claim only they have the solution. Don't vote for those who'd squander billions of dollars to protect plants and animals the Almighty already cares for. Don't spend so much energy saving the environment that you miss the Creator of that environment in the first place.

So, as a citizen of the kingdom, how should you approach the environment with Jesus Politics? Consider:

- Voting for politicians and policies that advance biblical environmentalism, that is, environmentalism that protects our God-given rights to cultivate, hunt, and use private land for the glory of the Almighty

- Shutting down the policies of environment worshippers, people who'd prioritize Mother Earth over Father God
- Doing your part to enjoy nature, using it to direct your attention and the attention of others to the Almighty

If you do these things, if you live by the principles of biblical environmentalism—even if it's a simple act like thanking God for a beautiful sunrise, taking a walk in the woods, saying grace over a vine-ripened tomato, or simply trusting that God cares more for his creation than you do—you'll find great peace and tranquility as you commune with the King in his garden. (Just as Jesus did on the mountainside.) You might also find yourself inviting others to recognize and enjoy the goodness of God's creation, drawing them closer to the King, just like I do every winter during duck season. And as you practice Jesus Politics as it relates to creation and the environment, see whether God doesn't do his part to hold this old world together without the passage of some Green New Deal.

God, thank you for giving us nature to enjoy, to provide for our needs, and to draw us closer to you. Help me to live by the principles of biblical environmentalism and trust that this world is ultimately under your control.

DAY 49 ★ PROTECTING HUMAN LIFE

You created my inmost being;
  you knit me together in my mother's womb.
I praise you because I am fearfully and wonderfully made.
—PSALM 139:13–14

There's not a doubt in my mind: Jesus wants nothing more than for all human life to be protected. And as people of the kingdom, we're supposed to value the things valued by our King. We're to love the people he'd love and protect the ones he'd protect, including unborn babies in their mothers' wombs. We're to make the King's desires known to our elected officials and demand and direct them in the way of preserving the dignity of unborn human life too. We're to use our votes to put people in office who will work to end this awful American genocide. And where our political action is ineffective, we're to use our time, money, and influence to persuade others to protect life. Just as Miss Kay does.

If ever there were a woman dedicated to ending abortion, it's Miss Kay. Time and time again, she counsels those who turn up pregnant to visit Life Choices Pregnancy Resource Center in Monroe, Louisiana, a place that offers hope to unexpected mothers. She often receives calls asking whether she'll intervene in the life of a mother who's considering abortion. Just a few weeks ago, Miss Kay told me about one such story.

On a typical Sunday afternoon, she received a call from a friend, a manager at a retail department store who'd overheard two women talking. One told the other she was pregnant, that it was unexpected. There was no support, the woman said. No money. No father to take care of the baby. And she was considering an abortion.

Miss Kay asked her friend to open up a conversation with the woman and invite her to visit Life Choices. The manager did just what

Miss Kay asked, and a few minutes later asked Miss Kay to meet her at the resource center in thirty minutes.

Miss Kay called Life Choices and found out they were getting ready to close for the day. Robertsons don't take no for an answer when it comes to human life, so Miss Kay told the woman on the line that closing wasn't an option. A life was on the line, and she expected a counselor who could perform an ultrasound to be there when she showed up in a few minutes. The woman at the center agreed and said she'd find a tech as soon as she could. So Miss Kay grabbed her keys and headed to town.

Sure enough, the manager and expectant mom showed up at Life Choices shortly after Miss Kay arrived. The pregnant woman shared her fear and confusion. Miss Kay and the folks at the center assured her there were resources available to help her carry the baby to term and keep the baby. And if she didn't want to keep the baby, there were people who would love to adopt a newborn. The woman listened and agreed to an ultrasound, and they all heard the heartbeat. And that was that. The woman made up her mind. How could she execute something with a heartbeat?

A citizen of the kingdom had overheard a conversation influenced by the evil one and sprang to action. The result was one less life added to the genocide census; one more life given the opportunity to commune with the Almighty. It was grassroots action, action that upheld the values of the King.

God, you are the Author of life, and you value every unborn baby you knit together in the womb. Help me to use my time, money, and influence to protect these little ones you love.

DAY 50 ★ SIMPLE HEALTHCARE

I pray that you may enjoy good health and that all may go
well with you, even as your soul is getting along well.
—3 JOHN V. 2

I was reared in the 1950s in a rural home. There were nine of us in
the Robertson camp in those days, and our access to healthcare was
limited. Maybe even more limited than the average American family.
We lived miles outside of town in a log cabin, and aside from the yearly
worm medication, we tended to our own ailments for the most part.
We had no health insurance. Not many did in those days. No way to
pay for regular doctor's visits. Instead, we relied on simple remedies.
A bottle of milk of magnesia for heartburn and constipation. A little
Mercurochrome or Dr. Tichenor's for a skinned knee. Tape for a cut
that wouldn't close up. Folk remedies for everything else.

Sure, there were times when milk of magnesia or Mercurochrome
or tape wouldn't do. And in those instances, Mom would load us up
and haul us to the clinic. There, the doctor would tend to the wound
or the broken limb. And when he was finished, he'd charge us a buck
and send us on our way. There was no paperwork. Very little hassle.

We couldn't afford to take medical care for granted in those days,
and neither could our neighbors. If someone had an infection or a cold
or injured themselves, the community pulled together and helped out
where they could. A good neighbor might bring a homemade poultice
or salve or some chicken soup to the house to help speed up the healing process. They might tend to their neighbor's garden or livestock
or fishing nets for a day or two if a particularly rough bout of influ-
enza came around. Neighbors helped neighbors in times of hardship.
I guess you could say the community was the safety net when the
worst illnesses hit, and we were both recipients of and participants in
that safety net.

I was a pretty hard-boned kid, and my immune system was firing on all cylinders, so I made my way through childhood without too many visits to the doctor and without much need for the community safety net. I graduated from high school, married Miss Kay, and moved on to college without any thought of buying health insurance. Sure, we visited the doctor and hospital from time to time when Miss Kay was pregnant, but it was still affordable. And truth be told, outside of the birth of our kids, we didn't have much use for the medical community. Between our home remedies and the kindness of our neighbors, we got along just fine. But while we were accustomed to making it with more rudimentary healthcare practices, the attitude in the country was changing.

Folks in this country began to see healthcare as a necessity, one right up there with food, clothing, and shelter. The healthcare industry took note, and prices for treatment began to rise. Politicians used the people's changing attitudes toward healthcare to leverage their own political power. In 2010, Obamacare required every citizen to buy health insurance, whether through their employer or on a government-facilitated exchange. With this new law, we took one step closer to becoming a full-blown nanny state. And because those plans were as expensive as all get-out, more and more Americans called for universal government-provided healthcare.

See how socialism creeps up on you?

* * *

God, thank you for the miracle of the human body and the wisdom you give to care for our ailments and wounds. Help me to take care of my loved ones and be a good neighbor to those in need.

DAY 51 ★ CHRIST'S ETERNAL HEALTHCARE PLAN

"He himself bore our sins" in his body
on the cross, so that we might die to
sins and live for righteousness; "by his
wounds you have been healed."
—1 PETER 2:24

King Jesus, the eternal Word of God, knew human sin created a barrier between us and God, and that because of sin, each of us would be subject to disease, death, and ultimately the judgment. So he came down from heaven and walked among us, living a perfect and sin-free life. At the end of his ministry, he offered himself in a great exchange, giving himself to the political authorities and suffering an unjust death on a cross to pay for our sins. Quoting the prophet Isaiah, the apostle Peter laid out the effect of Christ's crucifixion: "'He himself bore our sins' in his body on the cross, so that we might die to sins and live for righteousness; 'by his wounds you have been healed'" (1 Peter 2:24).

Healed from what? From spiritual disease, the disease that doesn't just infect our bodies but our souls. But it's not just spiritual disease he came to heal us from, and before you think I'm selling some sort of faith-healing mumbo jumbo, think again. The kind of physical healing Jesus brought might not be what you think.

After Jesus' death, he was laid in a tomb for three days. At the end of those three days, he conquered death, rising in a perfected body. He walked around in that body for a few weeks, spending time with his disciples before returning to heaven. The apostle Paul recorded that truth:

What I received I passed on to you as of first importance: that Christ died for our sins according to the Scriptures, that he was buried, that he was raised on the third day according to the Scriptures, and that he appeared to Cephas, and then to the Twelve. (1 Cor. 15:3–5)

What impact does his death and resurrection have on our physical bodies? Paul made it plain:

But Christ has indeed been raised from the dead, the firstfruits of those who have fallen asleep. For since death came through a man, the resurrection of the dead comes also through a man. For as in Adam all die, so in Christ all will be made alive. (vv. 20–22)

See there? Christ doesn't just offer forgiveness of sins and freedom from guilt and shame. He offers a way to beat physical death and the grave, to raise to new life with a new and incorruptible body. Now there's something the politicians in Washington, DC could never give you.

Freedom from sin, shame, and death? Resurrection from the grave? Could you have dreamed up such promises? Not me, dude. And this is why I've put my faith in Christ's eternal healthcare plan, the only healthcare plan that guarantees freedom from sin and shame, resurrection from the grave, and an eternity of disease-free living. This is why I preach it everywhere I go.

The way I see it, America, it all comes down to this. Who are you going to put your trust in? Are you going to place your health in the hands of a bunch of bureaucrats with no medical experience, who have no plan to foot the bill, and who cannot solve your most pressing healthcare concern (death), or will you place your health in the hands of the King of kings, the Lord Jesus who can save you from the grave and raise you to eternal health?

Seems like a no-brainer if you ask me.

★   ★   ★

God, thank you for forgiving my sins and giving me eternal life. While I make wise choices to take care of my body, help me to place my most pressing healthcare concern in your hands, knowing that you will ultimately save me from the grave and raise me to eternal health.

DAY 52 ★ HELPING OUR NEIGHBORS

Love your neighbor as yourself.
—MARK 12:31

As citizens of the King, as followers of Jesus Politics, we need to be clear. We need to share how government-run healthcare is just a front for the taxpayers' funding of immoral behavior. We need to share about eternal healthcare everywhere we go. We need to show the people that what they ultimately want—a solution for pain and death—can only be found in King Jesus.

As we speak out, we need to be proactive too. We need to help our neighbors as we can, help foot a medical bill here and there. Our churches ought to reach into the community and care for the sick. After all, it was King Jesus who said we ought to love our neighbors as ourselves:

> One of the teachers of the law came and heard them debating. Noticing that Jesus had given them a good answer, he asked him, "Of all the commandments, which is the most important?"
>
> "The most important one," answered Jesus, "is this: 'Hear, O Israel: The Lord our God, the Lord is one. Love the Lord your God with all your heart and with all your soul and with all your mind and with all your strength.' The second is this: 'Love your neighbor as yourself.' There is no commandment greater than these." (Mark 12:28–31)

It was also King Jesus who said that as we serve the down and out, we serve him (Matt. 25:40). So if you see your neighbor hurting, if you know of his healthcare needs, meet them as best you can. If enough of us did that, if we meet the needs of one another, there will be no need for government healthcare. And don't you think the watching world would take notice? Don't you think it'd make us true ambassadors for the Almighty?

So as citizens of the kingdom, let's advance Jesus Politics. Consider the following:

- Vote for those who will keep the government out of the medical system so they cannot advance a godless agenda (including requiring taxpayer funding of abortions or morning-after pills).
- Support politicians and policies that fight for a free-market healthcare system, the only kind of system that will be responsive to the paying public.
- Preach the importance of eternal healthcare everywhere you go.
- Get involved at the grassroots level, helping your neighbor when a medical need arises.

America, let's trust the right entity for our healthcare, the only one who can save us from sin, shame, death, and disease. Let's go all in on his eternal healthcare plan and invite our neighbors to participate with us. And let's call this movement for socialized medicine what it is: a scheme to get American Christians to foot the bill for death.

Lord, help me to advance your kingdom by supporting healthcare that promotes life, not death. May I take action to care for the sick in my community by helping my neighbors when medical needs arise.

DAY 53 ★ THE POWER OF FORGIVENESS

Be kind and compassionate to one another, forgiving each other, just as in Christ God forgave you.
—EPHESIANS 4:32

Years ago, my family went to New York City on a promotional tour. Jase had booked a room at the Trump International Hotel, and as he walked in, he asked a staff member where the bathroom was. Now by all objective measures, Jase might be the scraggliest of our bunch, and without his wife, Missy, by his side, he must have looked completely out of place. If I had my guess, that particular hotel employee had watched his fair share of training videos and likely had plenty of experience with the homeless population of Manhattan. He knew just what to do when he saw Jase.

With a smile and a nod, the gentleman ushered Jase down a hallway. They went through one door. Then another. The polite employee opened a third door, and it wasn't until it closed behind Jase that it dawned on him. He'd been escorted out through the rear entrance of the building.

Jase walked back around to the front of the building and found us waiting in the lobby. He told us what happened.

"I think I just got kicked out."

We looked at him in disbelief and then he added, "I think it was a case of *facial* profiling."

The joke sent the whole family into an uproar. So when the cameras rolled on *Live with Kelly and Michael*, Jase led with the story. There was no animosity in the way he told it. He hadn't demanded an apology or made a fuss about it. In fact, he laughed it off with the rest of us. He'd forgiven the employee the minute he'd gotten the boot.

Back in those days, anything a Robertson did made the news, and the story of Jase being treated as a vagrant at the Trump hotel was no exception. But the story was made all the more significant by the fact that another celebrity—someone bigger than any of us—had been mistreated in a similar fashion. She'd been shopping in Europe when she was refused access to an almost $40,000 purse. Did she let it go? Nah. She blew it up, made a big deal out of it.

And so when the news of Jase's hotel removal hit the news, there were two stories standing in stark contrast, and the bloggers and other media types took notice. One celebrity—Jase—had extended forgiveness for a misunderstanding when he'd been offended. The other had not.

I guess someone in the Trump organization must have been watching the television that morning. A manager reached out to Jase and apologized for the misunderstanding. Jase took that in stride and told them he didn't harbor any anger or bitterness. It was all understandable, he said. And this response made it back to Donald Trump Jr., who called to thank Jase for his graciousness.

It was a little example of the power of forgiveness, a funny story. But as I thought about it all years later, I considered how cultivating an attitude of mercy and forgiveness shapes our lives. It was a story that demonstrated how extending mercy and forgiveness leads to open doors and presents opportunities to share the good news of Jesus Christ. Forgiveness. Could forgiveness be the single most effective way of advancing Jesus Politics, particularly in such a vitriolic age?

God, thank you for forgiving my sins. Help me to extend that forgiveness to others, knowing that the power of forgiveness leads to opportunities to share the good news of Jesus Christ.

DAY 54 ★ FORGIVENESS AND MERCY IN POLITICS

Be merciful, just as your Father is merciful.
—LUKE 6:36

Forgiveness and mercy are in short supply these days, especially when it comes to politics. The anger, name-calling, and stone-throwing seems to be at an all-time high. Few extend the benefit of the doubt anymore. It doesn't take a court of law to declare you guilty, and when you're convicted in the court of public opinion, you're dismissed and declared unworthy of mercy or forgiveness. And if you don't know what I mean, you aren't keeping up with the news.

In 2018, I watched as a nominee to the Supreme Court, Brett Kavanaugh, suffered through an attempted political assassination. Since he was a conservative federal judge, I figured those on the Left would raise his pro-life record and might attack his stance on universal healthcare or the environment. I figured some would say he was too conservative. But I didn't expect they'd dig up dirt from his high school days and try to use it against him.

That September, Christine Blasey Ford came forward with incredible accusations. She alleged Kavanaugh had locked her in a room and sexually assaulted her when both of them were in high school. Kavanaugh denied the allegations, saying they were a political hit by left-wingers. The media took sides, of course. Left-wing outlets attacked Kavanaugh, and right-wing outlets attacked Blasey Ford. The commentators went nuts. They resorted to name-calling, finger-pointing, and character assassination. And all of this happened in the wide-open public because of an allegation of behavior that was supposed to have happened thirty-five years ago.

Brett Kavanaugh was ultimately confirmed and now sits on the

Supreme Court. And to be clear, I make no claim as to whether he is guilty or innocent of anything he's been accused of. I won't cast any aspersions at Blasey Ford, either. I only highlight this story to show how the lack of mercy, grace, and forgiveness disrupts the political process and draws our attention away from the real issues plaguing our country.

I don't spend much time on the internet or social media, but I watch enough cable news to know the debate and dialogue out there is merciless. Politicians and constituents fight, cuss, and spit at one another, using the mistakes and sins of the past against others in order to gain political power. Often, they don't give a rip about the facts. They believe the worst without extending an ounce of grace or understanding.

Now don't get me wrong, if Justice Kavanaugh or any other politician broke the law, and if the evidence leads to a conviction and sentencing, then they ought to be held accountable for their crimes. But short of that, all this bickering and fighting isn't good for our country. Digging up thirty-five-year-old sins and blasting it across the media might make for good television, but what does it really accomplish? Does it help us solve any problems facing our country or does it only serve as a distraction from the issues that really matter? And so, America, the way I see it, we need a new way of speaking in the political arena. We need a new way of dealing with our political opponents. We need to act as Jesus would if he were engaged in our current political climate.

★   ★   ★

Jesus, help me to behave the way you would act if you were engaged in modern American politics. Help me to consider the facts and extend grace, understanding, and forgiveness as needed.

DAY 55 ★ THE FORGIVENESS OF JESUS

Father, forgive them, for they do not know what they are doing.
—LUKE 23:34

I haven't lived the most spotless life. In fact, for the first two decades of my life, I was pretty unruly. So if you wanted to drag a skeleton out of my closet from all those years ago, it wouldn't take you long to find one. Truth be told, I've dragged out plenty of my own skeletons over the years in an effort to be honest about who I was before the Almighty got hold of me. But when I walked into the saving work of the Almighty, I found a God who forgave every sin and dealt with me in great mercy. I found a church full of people who did the same, who didn't hold my past sins against me. Why were these people so forgiving and kind to me? They followed the way of King Jesus.

Forgiveness doesn't come to us naturally. It's something that's learned as it's experienced. To put it another way, to learn forgiveness, we have to be forgiven. And there's no better way to learn and experience forgiveness than to look at the life of King Jesus, the man who went to the cross to wipe away all our sins.

King Jesus could have put all his political foes to shame. He could have outed all their sins, even the hidden ones, and used it to climb the ranks of power. But God with Us came with a different purpose in mind. He came to forgive us, to free us from the sin and shame of everything we've done and everything we'll do. This is the good news of Jesus.

Time and time again, Jesus' ministry was marked by forgiveness and mercy, and he called others to extend that same forgiveness and mercy. Need proof? Consider these passages:

- In the Sermon on the Mount, Jesus warned the people: "For if you forgive men their trespasses, your heavenly Father will also forgive you. But if you do not forgive men their trespasses, neither will your Father forgive your trespasses" (Matt. 6:14–15 NKJV).

- When the religious leaders caught a woman in adultery, when they threatened to stone her on the spot, Jesus said, "Let any one of you who is without sin be the first to throw a stone at her" (John 8:7). Then he forgave her sins.
- When Peter asked how many times he ought to forgive the sins of his neighbor, when he offered "up to seven times?" Jesus responded. "Not seven times," he said, "but seventy-seven times" (Matt. 18:21–22).
- And what was one of Christ's last acts on the cross? He looked down on his opponents, the men who crucified him, and spoke these words over them: "Father, forgive them, for they do not know what they are doing" (Luke 23:34).

Jesus was not quick to cast stones. He didn't attack his opponents, political or otherwise. He didn't accuse the accusers. Instead, he extended forgiveness and grace to all.

Does this mean King Jesus let everything go, that he didn't take hard stands on the issues? Hardly. He didn't tolerate sin, and he preached some hard words about lust and anger and greed and gossip and the like. But time and time again, when the people fell short, Jesus picked them up, dusted them off, and forgave them, sometimes when they didn't even ask him to.

★ ★ ★

Lord, thank you for forgiving me and setting me free from sin and shame. Help me to stay true to your Word while extending your forgiveness and mercy to others.

DAY 56 ★ THE ROLE OF FORGIVENESS AND MERCY

Bear with each other and forgive one another if any of you has a grievance against someone. Forgive as the Lord forgave you.
—COLOSSIANS 3:13

As followers of King Jesus, as citizens of the kingdom, we're called to be like him. Yes, we're to take a hard line on sin, debauchery, and lawlessness. We're to call folks in the world around us to repentance and invite them into kingdom living. But how do we do this? Not through name-calling or by lording the past over our opponents. Instead, we're to be quick to extend mercy and forgiveness, slow to judge. It won't always be easy, particularly when folks on the other side of the political spectrum try to drag us to the bottom of the barrel when they drag out the past of our political leaders in an attempt to destroy us. It won't be easy when we uncover decades-old dirt on our political opponents either, dirt that might give us an advantage in an upcoming election. But still, as followers of King Jesus, as citizens of the kingdom, we're to engage our opponents—including our political opponents—as he did. With mercy and forgiveness.

Now, don't hear what I'm not saying. Extending mercy and forgiveness to our political opponents doesn't mean there aren't consequences for sin, particularly sins committed by politicians while holding public office. If a sitting Supreme Court justice has broken the laws of the land, you'd better believe there should be consequences. If a president lies or obstructs justice while holding office (particularly if there's evidence to back up the claim), then he or she should be held accountable. Even, still, you can only dole out these consequences with a sober and forgiving spirit. You can remove a man from office without hate and vitriol. Ultimately, you can hope the consequences of his sin humble him and lead him to repentance. And if it does, the citizens of the King can be there, waiting, ready to show him mercy and lead him to the Almighty who removes every sin and every consequence.

So as you enter into political debate during an election cycle, discuss the issues plaguing our country. But as you do, ask yourself:

- Do I forgive those who represent opposing political viewpoints the way I'd want to be forgiven?
- Would I hold a politician's distant past against them in order to gain a political advantage?
- Do I speak with the same mercy and forgiveness I'd want my politicians to demonstrate?
- Do I demand that my leaders extend mercy and forgiveness to their political opponents, that they show civility in the way they carry out the day-to-day business of governing?

If the answer to these questions is no, do something about it. Refuse to attack a politician for his past shortcomings while still attacking ungodly political positions. And sit down with those you might not agree with and debate the issues. Debate them vociferously. But as you do, do it as Jesus might, without all the hate, anger, and mercilessness that's prevalent today in our society. And when your political allies and opponents ask why you're willing to extend mercy and understanding to those on the other side of the aisle, tell them it's because you're engaged in Jesus Politics. You're trying your best to forgive as he forgave, even while toeing the kingdom line. See what kind of doors it might open.

★　　★　　★

Jesus, show me how to extend mercy and understanding to those on the other side of the political aisle. Help me to forgive those who represent opposing political viewpoints and speak with mercy toward others as I hold fast to your truth.

DAY 57 ★ WE CARRY THE LAW OF LOVE

If you really keep the royal law found in Scripture,
"Love your neighbor as yourself," you are doing right.
—JAMES 2:8

The kingdom of God has come, and we are ambassadors of the King. We are subject to its law, the law of love, and that law is higher than any bill passed by the legislators in Washington or any other state of the Union. The law of the kingdom of God is outside the jurisdiction of the United States Supreme Court too.

Practically speaking, what does this mean for those who want to follow King Jesus?

- When the Supreme Court affirms laws allowing abortion on demand, the people of the kingdom should resist, demonstrating love toward the unborn baby and his or her mother.
- When any legislative body changes the definition of marriage, the people of the kingdom should call their politicians, judges, and neighbors to repent and to love, honor, and cherish their spouse of the opposite sex all the way to death.
- When any arm of the government tries to cram some godless, unconstitutional law into our lives, the citizens of the kingdom should respond in love, calling our country to repent.

As you're repenting, also begin serving the King by serving others and calling your neighbors to repent. You'll be able to watch as they find new freedom. Freedom from lust and runaway sexual desire? Sure, because all our desires will be met in the spouses we love, the spouses the King has given us. Freedom from anger, hate, and violence? You bet, because the love of the King will cast out all violence. Freedom from the chains of death that plague us all? That's the best part of living by the law of love.

And for a moment just imagine a world changed by the law of love practiced among the people. Wouldn't our country be so much different? Our abortion rates, divorce rates, suicide rates, murder rates, sexually transmitted disease rates—wouldn't they drop to something near zero? Would we spend so much of our time debating healthcare if we provided for our sick neighbors like we provide for ourselves, if the big pharmaceutical companies were run by people who loved the King? Would we continue to hear of mass shootings in the news? Nah. How do I know? Just ask yourself: *When's the last time a godly person, a Jesus-loving Christian who lives by the Bible, shot up a school?*

When we live by the law of the King, the law of love, we bring natural order to our lives. And if enough of us did that, if enough of us traded our political ideologies for Jesus Politics, the face of America would change.

★　　★　　★

King Jesus, thank you for your law of love, which casts out anger, hatred, and violence. Help me to carry this law of love into all areas of my life as I serve others, call my neighbors to repent, and celebrate as they find new freedom in you.

DAY 58 ★ KINGDOM LIVING

Remind the people to be subject to rulers and authorities, to be obedient, to be ready to do whatever is good.
—TITUS 3:1

King Jesus came preaching the truth, but he also fed the people, healed diseases, raised the dead, and set free those who were trapped in religious shackles. The agenda of the King was to do good everywhere he went and, through it, to break the evil one's hold on people's hearts and to invite them into a new way of living, namely, kingdom living.

Teach, preach, and do good. This could have been the kingdom-living slogan of the early church. It wasn't just Peter who used it either. In his letter to Titus, Paul encouraged the church to do good:

- Titus was to set an example for the young men of the church "by *doing what is good*" (2:7).
- The entire church was to be "eager to *do what is good*" (2:14).
- Those who trusted in God were to "be careful to devote themselves to *doing what is good*" (3:8).
- Paul closed the letter: "Our people must learn to devote themselves to *doing what is good*, in order to provide for urgent needs and not live unproductive lives" (3:14).

As far as Paul was concerned, followers of the King were to be outspoken and live action-oriented lives, lives worthy of the King. But how did he describe those who didn't live lives worthy of the King? He wrote: "They claim to know God, but by their actions they deny him. They are detestable, disobedient and unfit for doing anything good" (1:16).

It ain't rocket science, America. In fact, it's so simple it might be called *redneck* science. If we follow God in teaching, preaching, and doing good, we'll be blessed. If we don't? If we turn our backs on God's good and follow our own desires, we'll reap an ungodly harvest of murder, death, and destruction.

So as you consider the platform positions of the world versus those of Jesus Politics, ask yourself which sounds like doing good:

- The government's interference with our right to worship the Almighty *or* allowing people to practice their faith in the public sector?
- Taking away a democratic people's ability to fight against tyranny without addressing the hate in the human heart *or* standing up for the rights established by our Founding Fathers?
- Elevating the creation over the Creator *or* worshipping the Creator before creation?
- Terminating human life *or* saving human life?
- Is it good to deprive a child of both a mother and father *or* is it better to protect God's definition of marriage?
- Is asking the government to provide high-cost, unsustainable, temporary healthcare good *or* is it better to seek eternal healthcare and then chip in to provide for the needs of your neighbor?

I could go on and on, but the idea of preaching, teaching, and doing good goes well beyond the platform issues of Jesus Politics. It involves practical things, too, like serving our neighbors and inviting them over. Doing good might mean creating jobs for our unemployed neighbors or giving them interest-free loans for a medical need. It means sharing the good news of Jesus with them, and when they move on it, inviting them into the waters of baptism.

Doing good means loving our neighbors. That's what the King did, and imitating him is the way to go.

★   ★   ★

Lord, help me to practice kingdom living by teaching, preaching, and doing good. Give me opportunities to take action by serving others and sharing with them your good news.

DAY 59 ★ TAKING KINGDOM LIVING TO THE STREET

He has shown you, O mortal, what is good.
  And what does the Lord require of you?
To act justly and to love mercy
  and to walk humbly with your God.
—MICAH 6:8

Miss Kay and I are what some might call community activists, although we just call ourselves followers of the King. We work with the down and out, the drunks, the drug addicts, and those mired in sexual sin, regardless of color, creed, or sexual orientation. We deal with the people most Americans wouldn't give the time of day to. We welcome folks who carry everything they own in a backpack or, if they're really well off, an old clunker of a car. We welcome the wealthy too. And in our neck of the woods, we've gained a reputation for it. (It bears mentioning that many others in our local community have the same reputation for kingdom living.)

Among those folks who've made their way down to the river was a young, evidently struggling woman who looked like she hadn't eaten in weeks. Bone thin, hair almost as wild as my beard, she walked into our church a few years ago and sat in front of me and Miss Kay for an entire service. After the closing hymn and prayer, she turned to me and said, "Mr. Robertson, could you help me?"

I took one look at her. Strung out. Helpless. Probably not a dime to her name. I was moved with compassion.

"Sure," I said. "Let's gather a few of my friends and talk it out."

And that's exactly what we did.

To a circle of my most trusted friends, she explained how she'd had just enough for a bus ticket from Arizona, how she wanted to make her way to the Robertson family because she'd seen *Duck Dynasty* and thought maybe we could give her some answers. She shared about her heroin use, how the drug had its hooks in her, and how she needed a way out. Could we help?

Sure we could, I told her. But she'd need to do a few things. She'd need a rehab bed for a few weeks, and then she'd need a place to land when she got out. She'd need to find a job and hold it down, something that could instill her with a little dignity. More than any of that, though, she'd need a faith to hold onto. She'd need the stability that only a King can bring.

She listened and followed the advice my friends and I gave her. She cleaned up, got a job, and became a child of the King. Miss Kay put her up in a rental house. We found her a beat-up but serviceable vehicle. She worked the plan and found so much freedom.

Freedom from drugs? Yes.

Freedom from welfare and government assistance? Yes.

Freedom from sin and death and ultimately the grave? You bet.

Sometime after her recovery, she sent a note to me through Miss Kay. It was a simple note of gratitude: "Mr. Robertson, thank you for giving me hope."

Lord, help me to take kingdom living to the streets. Show me how to share your love and the resources you have entrusted to me with those around me who need freedom and hope.

DAY 60 ★ HOPE FOR THE HOPELESS

May the God of hope fill you with all joy and peace
as you trust in him, so that you may overflow
with hope by the power of the Holy Spirit.
—ROMANS 15:13

Hope for the hopeless. That's what happens when followers of the King carry his message to the world without reservation. That's what happens when we're unashamed of the good news of Jesus.

Jesus Politics is about more than changing government structures and systems. Jesus Politics is about loving the King so much that you'd go out of your way to share that love with your neighbors. King Jesus himself said this is what life is all about. He taught, "'Love the Lord your God with all your heart and with all your soul and with all your mind.' This is the first and greatest commandment. And the second is like it: 'Love your neighbor as yourself'" (Matt. 22:37–39).

If we truly love our neighbors, won't we share the way of the King with them? And if we love America, won't we do whatever we can to preserve our freedoms to share that love?

No matter where I go, no matter what I do, I keep my eyes and ears tuned to the loving work of the King. Sometimes that work takes me to a place where I address political issues, where I do my part to speak out about abortion or religious liberty or the Second Amendment or healthcare or whatever. Sometimes it takes me to the grass roots though, to those who need help getting off drugs, off the welfare roll, and off the hit list of the evil one. And when those opportunities come up, I move on them. In love. Why? Because I'm a servant of the King, called to live out my life just as he would.

Remember this: Jesus Politics is not about supporting a particular political agenda. Jesus Politics isn't just meant to give you debate points or talking points for those social media sites everyone seems

131

to love these days. It's not even just about what you do in the voting booth. Ultimately, Jesus Politics is about loving God, loving our neighbors, and doing whatever it takes to bring, maintain, and protect his kingdom on earth as it is in heaven.

Followers of the King, whether in Northern Louisiana, Southern California, or New York City, let's get out there and do our thing. Let's take our kingdom manifesto to the streets, showing the world the difference a bunch of King worshippers can make. If enough of us do, if we stay the course, the history books will tell of the era in which America was almost lost. Those same books will record how a small but mighty band of believers fought for what was right, took Jesus Politics to the streets, and won back the soul of America. And when our children, grandchildren, and great-grandchildren read those history books to their own children, they'll remember the manifesto of their ancestors, folks who might be called the Re-Founding Fathers and Mothers. They'll remember our battle cry, and they'll make it their own: All hail the King!

★ ★ ★

King Jesus, thank you for saving me and calling me to kingdom living. Help me to love you, love my neighbors, and do whatever it takes to bring, maintain, and protect your kingdom on earth as it is in heaven.

★ *PART IV* ★

FAITH

THEREFORE, SINCE WE HAVE BEEN JUSTIFIED
THROUGH FAITH, WE HAVE PEACE WITH
GOD THROUGH OUR LORD JESUS CHRIST.

—ROMANS 5:1

DAY 61 ★ THE POWER OF THE GOSPEL

I am not ashamed of the gospel, because it is the power
of God that brings salvation to everyone who believes.
—ROMANS 1:16

Miss Kay gave me the address to her apartment and asked me to
meet her there at five o'clock. The preacher, Bill Smith, would
be there, she said.

That night Bill sat across from me at Miss Kay's makeshift dinner
table and asked a pointed question.

"What do you think of when you hear the word *gospel*, Phil?"

"I don't know," I said. "The Chuck Wagon Gang? Gospel music?"

"Do you know the good news?" he asked.

The good news of what? I'd been to church, but I'd never really
heard what could be called *good news*. I'd heard the stories of the Old
Testament characters. I'd been told I needed to hear, believe, repent,
confess, and be baptized, but every time I heard this formula, I was left
thinking, *Hear what? Believe what? Repent from what? Confess what?*
No, I told Bill, to the best of my recollection I'd never heard any good
news in church. Instead, I was given a do-right formula, and I never
felt like I could do right. I wasn't good enough.

"I see," he said. "Can I tell you the best news you've ever heard?"

I nodded.

Bill drew a series of hieroglyphs on a folded napkin. First, he drew
an arrow pointing down. Then a cross. Next a half circle. Then an
arrow pointing up. Finally, he drew an arrow pointing down.

"Let's keep it simple," he said, then he shared how God made man
for fellowship, but how man broke God's law. As a consequence, men

had been separated from God ever since. "But God never wanted that separation," he said, "and so he made a way."

He pointed to the first arrow and explained how the God who created the universe loved man enough to step into that creation. Jesus was God's very Word made flesh, he said, and Jesus came and lived among his people. He healed the sick, made the lame walk, and brought provision to the poor. That same Jesus preached the ultimate good news: those who followed him would be free from sin and guilt and would have an eternal home with him.

Bill pointed to the cross he'd drawn on the napkin, then explained how Jesus' teachings made the religious folks so angry they nailed him to a cross. When Jesus went to the cross, he took on the sins of the whole world. He took on the penalty of our separation.

Then Bill pointed to the semicircle, the dome. After his death Jesus was laid in a tomb, Bill said. He pointed to the next arrow, the arrow pointing up, and he laid out the scriptures showing how Jesus conquered death, how he rose from the dead. The final arrow showed how Christ would return for those who believed.

"He's coming back for his people, for those who've trusted in his death, burial, and resurrection," Bill said. "Then he'll take us home to live with him in eternity."

I sat there, stunned. I'd gone to church for years. How had I missed this? God could forgive me? He could free me from sin and guilt, even with all the things I'd done? He'd allow me to live in eternity with him? It was the most compelling story I'd ever heard. This was truly good news!

★ ★ ★

Jesus, thank you for the gospel—that you came to earth and died on the cross to take the penalty of my sins so that, when I put my faith in you, I can be free from sin and guilt and have eternal life in heaven! The gospel is truly the most compelling, powerful story ever told.

DAY 62 ★ A NEW CREATION

Therefore, if anyone is in Christ, the new creation has come: The old has gone, the new is here!
—2 CORINTHIANS 5:17

That same night, I reviewed the scriptures Bill had referenced. I read the first chapter of the Gospel of John, and sure enough, there it was. The very living God—the God who was surely not dead—came to earth in the form of Jesus. I read of his life, his death, and his resurrection. In Paul's writings I came to understand that Jesus had died as a sacrifice for my sins. It was this sacrifice that made a way for me (1 Cor. 15:3–5).

I read the promises of John, how choosing to be in fellowship with Jesus would free me from all sins—past, present, and future. Finally, in the book of Acts, I read the ultimate promise. Jesus would return for everyone who believed in him.

Sure enough, the story was just as Bill said. The Bible showed how God was very much alive, and how he made a way for forgiveness of my sin. He could free me of all my guilt and could solve my ultimate problem—death. The notion of freedom from guilt and death filled me with great peace, a peace of mind I'd never experienced. I knew this story was the solution to all my problems. It was the solution to my disorienting drunkenness, my promiscuity, my search for freedom. And the more I considered it, the more I came to see that it satisfied a deep spiritual longing I didn't even know I had.

I met with Bill the next evening and told him I'd done my homework. I'd reviewed every scripture he gave me, and sure enough, his story panned out. It was the greatest story I'd ever heard, I said, and I wanted to follow this Jesus. I wanted to be baptized.

That night, in a near-empty auditorium with Bill Smith, Miss Kay, and my three boys, I gave my confession of faith. I believed in the saving work of Jesus and wanted to be free of sin and guilt. I wanted to follow him in baptism. Down into the water I went, and when I came up from that cleansing flood, I knew I was a changed man. Somehow, in that water, I'd encountered God. And that was the moment I decided I'd share the good news of Jesus with anyone God put in my path.

I stepped out of that baptistery, made my way to Miss Kay and the boys, and gave each of them a soggy hug. There was a new joy in this embrace with Miss Kay; a shift was already happening. The peace and strength I'd seen in Miss Kay over those last two days began to fill me too. Everything seemed so much lighter. And though I wasn't sure how I'd stay on the straight and narrow, shaky as I was, I figured God would make a way. Wasn't this the promise of all those scriptures I'd studied?

God, I praise you for your free gift of salvation, which makes me a new creation! Thank you for forgiving my sins and offering me a brand-new start, so I can follow you and your ways.

DAY 63 ★ THE ONLY HOPE FOR MANKIND

And everyone who calls
on the name of the Lord will be saved.
—ACTS 2:21

Years later Bill Smith told me that our meeting at Miss Kay's apartment convinced him to begin sharing the good news of God through that same little diagram he showed me. He called it "The Witness," and for years he carried it with him everywhere he went. The church had it translated into multiple languages, and missionaries shared it around the world. It's proven to be a powerful tool and, following Bill's example, I still share it with anyone God brings to me: the rich, the poor, the powerless and powerful.

In 2016, just before the presidential election, I had the privilege of meeting with then presidential nominee Donald Trump in Washington, DC, at the Values Voter Summit. There I asked whether I could share some good news with him. He agreed, and I pulled out a copy of The Witness I'd drawn on a card.

"Whether you win or lose, don't miss this," I said. "This is the most important thing you'll ever hear."

I explained the diagram and shared how the living God had made a way for us to have fellowship with him. I shared the truth of Jesus, of his death, burial, resurrection, and ascension. I shared how belief in Jesus might free him from all his past and future sins. I shared how he might come to live for eternity. When I finished, I looked up at him, wondering what he might say.

He pointed to the diagram, which I'd placed on his desk. "Can I have that?" he asked. I handed it to him, and he folded it up and put it in his pocket.

I don't know if President Trump had ever heard the truth of God before that day, and I don't know whether he has accepted the message I shared with him. But here's what I know: like all of us, God has written the truth of his law on the president's heart. And so, sooner or later (if he hasn't already), I pray that God sees fit to lead him into that truth. I hope President Trump has a freeing encounter with the God who is most certainly alive, the God who cannot be killed by human hands.

If there's one thing I know, it's this: an encounter with the living God is the only hope for mankind. It's the only hope for President Trump, for me, for America. It's the only hope for true freedom and lasting peace. And the God of the universe has made a way for us to have this kind of encounter. That way is Jesus, the very personification of God, the very hope of the world.

The personification—the one men believed they killed—defeated death. He is alive, no matter what the professors, psychologists, and scientists say.

★   ★   ★

God, you are no respecter of persons—you offer your gift of salvation to everyone. Thank you for your gospel, which is the only hope for mankind. Help me to be faithful to share this hope with others.

DAY 64 ★ GROWING IN FAITH

Like newborn babies, crave pure spiritual milk,
so that by it you may grow up in your salvation.
—1 PETER 2:2

I'd spent twenty-eight years under the influence of Satan. I knew it'd take time to untangle all those lies, and you can't untangle the lies of the Devil when you're running with his children. I knew what I needed to do, and I entered a self-imposed sort of holy witness protection program. We'd already moved, and the boys from Junction City didn't know where I was living. I changed my phone number. I cut off communication with the men who'd trained me to follow my own desires. I stopped running around with Big Al and the crew once and for all. I lived like a recluse, almost as if I were in hiding for the first three months.

In those reclusive days, Bill invited me to a Bible study with a rather prolific group of well-known sinners. In that study he taught us the truth about sin and the father of sin. The Devil, he said, was the father of lies, and he was prowling, looking for an opening to steal us back. He taught us that the only way to combat the lies of Satan was to devote ourselves to the study of Scripture and to allow God to speak through its pages.

And so I devoted the majority of my waking hours to studying the Bible. I pored over the onion-skin pages and began to mark them up. I consumed the Word of God as if it were food and drank deeply from its waters of wisdom. As I read and read and read, I saw the truth about the human condition: every last one of us has been infected by sin; every last one of us is under the influence of the evil one.

As Miss Kay and I righted the ship of our marriage, I decided I needed to leave the oil fields and put my education to work. I had two college degrees and classroom experience, but I'd lost my teaching job in Junction City on account of my wayward lifestyle. What's more, I had a record with the law, a thing that doesn't earn you any points with high school administrators when you're looking to steer the lives of the town's youth. But, resolved to make good, I went to my new church family and asked them to put in a good word. Bill Smith reached out to contacts he had at a Christian school in Ouachita Parish, and though they would not hire me for a permanent position, they allowed me to substitute teach. I worked hard, did the best I could, and before long I was hired as coach and literature teacher at Ouachita Christian School.

Things were changing. The power of God was active in my life. This power was awakening me to the truth of the gospel: in Jesus I could beat sin and death; in Jesus I could have a new life. It stripped me of my desire to go back to my old partying ways, sure. Even more, it set me on a path of understanding. And in that understanding, an unquenchable desire to free others began to grow in me.

God, thank you for your Word, which is living and active in my life. Fill me with your strength and wisdom as I study the Scriptures and learn how to honor and obey you.

DAY 65 ★ UNITY IS POSSIBLE

**For he himself is our peace, who has made the
two groups one and has destroyed the
barrier, the dividing wall of hostility.**
—EPHESIANS 2:14

The anger and fear, the name-calling and division spun up by so many politicians these days is not one-sided. Conservatives fall prey to it. Liberals fall prey to it. And insult by insult, brick by brick, we've built a strong and mighty wall between the two sides. With that wall firmly in place, unity has become a pipe dream.

But here's what I know from experience: walls can come down. Divisions can be repaired. Unity is possible through the saving message of Christ. How do I know? I've experienced it.

The gospel of Jesus found me when I was as poor as dirt and as redneck as they come. (For the record, only one of those things has changed.) Before my conversion to Christ, I didn't have a moral fiber in my body. I didn't run with business leaders or upstanding men of the community. I might not have known a single person who owned a suit. I consorted with one type of person—poor, hell-raising, duck-hunting, deer-poaching rednecks. What'd we think of those slick-suited business types who were different from us? Not much.

When I came into the church, everything changed. I still had my fair share of redneck friends, folks who lived on the blue-collar side of the tracks. But as I started attending Bible studies and church services, I started meeting folks from different socioeconomic classes. I met folks who were deadly serious about politics and those who weren't. I spent more time with bankers and business owners. And though I'd always known my fair share of African American folks—as a youngster, I'd picked cotton with many—this was the first time I was rubbing shoulders with them in the church congregation.

There, under the preaching of Bill Smith at the White's Ferry Road Church, I learned this truth of the gospel: in the family of God, there was no distinction between the sons and daughters of the Almighty. We were all equal. I might be a river rat. The man on my left might be a black factory worker. The fella to my right might be a white, suit-wearing banker. The woman in front of me might be a stay-at-home mom or a saleswoman or an attorney. We might have various political views (although the Bible calls us to agree on things like abortion and marriage). Under the gospel of Jesus, we'd been made part of the same family, Bill said. No one was more favored than any other.

This unifying message wasn't just talk at White's Ferry Road Church. The congregation took it as the gospel truth. They didn't ask me to shave my beard or clean up. They didn't ask me to adopt a certain political party or ideology. They took me as I was, scruffy and unshorn, sometimes a little odiferous, depending on whether I'd had chores to do that morning.

Don't get me wrong; we weren't perfect. Over the years a few folks at the church have lost sight of the truth. Time after time, though, we manage to come back to the truth of the gospel. The Almighty looks at the heart, and he wants us to be unified under his saving message. Couldn't our modern world use a dose of this message of unity?

God, thank you that there are no distinctions in your family. Help me to look past people's differences and embrace the unifying message of the gospel.

DAY 66 ★ THE WORD OF GOD WILL NOT FAIL

My word that goes out from my mouth:
    It will not return to me empty,
but will accomplish what I desire
    and achieve the purpose for which I sent it.
—ISAIAH 55:11

Just before the launch of *Duck Dynasty*, I attended the opening of a sporting goods store in Minnesota. The crowd looked like my kind of folks—hunters, fishermen, and trappers who wore camouflage and sported ample facial hair. I pulled my duck calls from my bag and performed my usual calling routine. Then, after giving what I believed to be a rousing presentation, I put the calls back into my bag and pulled out my Bible.

"Minnesota," I said, holding up the Good Book, "let me tell you about something more important than mallard calls."

I shared the good news of Jesus with those old boys, how he'd come making promises. He said he'd remove all our sins—past, present, and future. He said he'd free us from guilt and shame. He promised he'd raise our bodies from the grave. He'd give us a new and everlasting life, and if we follow his truth in this life, we'd be freed from the very real consequences of chasing after our sinful and lawless desires.

"Listen," I said, "I've tried the other way of living, including living under the rule of the king of beers. Let me tell you something: Following Jesus? It's the only way to roll."

With that, I exited the stage, made my way to the airport, and returned to Louisiana.

It was an engagement much like any other, and I didn't think much about it after the fact. That is, until about five years later when

Miss Kay came into the living room carrying a letter. "You need to read this," she said. It was from a name I didn't recognize, and the return address was from Minnesota.

It was a long letter from a man who'd attended the big-box store opening all those years ago. The writer had been offended by my gospel presentation. He said that in the years that followed, he'd made it his life's goal to dog-cuss me to anyone who'd listen.

But then, after years of living in all that hatred, something shifted. About four years into his personal vendetta, the old boy was mulling over how much he hated me, and as he did, he considered his life. It was a real mess, marked by anger, addiction, and the consequences of chasing after sin. He'd reexamined my message and came to a simple conclusion: I'd offered him the best news he'd ever heard, and he'd gone out of his way to hate me for it.

There in his living room, he wrote, he gave his life to Christ. He'd been baptized and had been living in the truth for more than a year. Everything I'd promised he'd found to be true, and he shared the message everywhere he went. Now he was writing a letter to apologize.

I put the letter back in the envelope and gave thanks for my new brother in Minnesota. He didn't need to apologize, of course. After all, I'd only done what I was instructed to do—go into the world preaching the good news and making disciples. And thanks to the Almighty, he'd come to know the truth, and the truth had set him free from all that hate. Now he worshiped everywhere he went.

This is what the truth does, see. It sets us free from sin, free to worship.

★　　★　　★

God, help me to be faithful to share the truth of Jesus at every opportunity and leave the rest in your hands. I know that you alone can save, and you are faithful to your Word.

DAY 67 ★ CHURCH IS MORE THAN A BUILDING

God is spirit, and his worshipers must worship in the Spirit and in truth.
—JOHN 4:24

Jesus never meant for his message to be contained within a building or confined to a service. He came to seek and save the lost, and where were the lost? They were out in the streets. The lost were the businessmen, the fishermen, the women working at home. The lost were the children running through the streets. The lost were the beggars, the crippled, and the leprous. They were the tax collectors, prostitutes, and sinners. So, although Jesus preached from time to time in the synagogue, he spent most of his time spreading his good news where the people were—in the world. In fact, Jesus was among the people so much that the religious teachers of the day took issue with it. They asked why he spent so much time with tax collectors and sinners. They called him a drunkard because he attended parties where sinners were. They watched as he spent time with women—women with bad reputations at that. Time and time again, they took issue with just how *in the world* Jesus was. But as Jesus went, he wasn't compartmentalizing his faith. He was out there preaching. And what was he preaching? Freedom.

Freedom from sin.

Freedom from death.

Freedom from religious obligation.

Freedom to worship the Almighty everywhere, all the time.

Take, for example, the story John told us in the fourth chapter of his gospel. After traveling throughout the region, Jesus and his disciples took a break in a Samaritan town. Sitting by the town well,

147

Jesus sent the disciples into town to buy food. While he waited, a Samaritan woman came to draw water, and Jesus struck up a conversation with her. He shared with her the best news—that he could satisfy her spiritual thirst. He also told her he knew everything about her life of sin. The woman was astounded and said, "Sir . . . I can see that you are a prophet" (4:19).

No kidding, gal!

Thinking Jesus might be able to answer the age-old Samaritan question of worship, she pointed up to the mountain across the way. "Our ancestors worshiped on this mountain," she said, "but you Jews claim that the place where we must worship is in Jerusalem" (v. 20).

It was a statement, but it carried an implied question. *Where am I supposed to worship the Almighty?* Jesus came to destroy the barrier between the temple and the streets, and his answer must have surprised her. He said,

> "A time is coming when you will worship the Father neither on this mountain nor in Jerusalem. . . . A time is coming and has now come when the true worshipers will worship the Father in the Spirit and in truth, for they are the kind of worshipers the Father seeks. God is spirit, and his worshipers must worship in the Spirit and in truth" (vv. 21–24).

Jesus couldn't have been any clearer. Worship of the Almighty wasn't meant to be hidden away within the four walls of a building. It wasn't meant to be compartmentalized or kept out of society. True worship—proclaiming God's glory and truth—happens everywhere the Christian goes. Why? Because the Christian is the very temple of the Almighty's Spirit.

★　★　★

God, you are never confined to a building or a service. Show your glory to the world through your people as we go out to serve and live for you.

DAY 68 ★ THE CHURCH ON THE GO

His intent was that now, through the church, the manifold wisdom of God should be made known to the rulers and authorities in the heavenly realms, according to his eternal purpose that he accomplished in Christ Jesus our Lord.
—EPHESIANS 3:10–11

The apostle Paul wrote that our worship is best expressed as we *go*. It is expressed best as we carry the good news of Jesus outside the walls of our churches and into the chaotic, dying world. It's expressed through our acts of service, hospitality, prayer, and hope. It's expressed by being *different* from the world. But how will the world see that difference if we're not actually out in the world? How do we serve the Lord's agenda if we hide within a church building? We don't.

In his letter to the Ephesians, Paul reminded the people that God no longer lives in temples. Instead, he wrote that the people of the church "are being built together to become a dwelling in which God lives by his Spirit" (2:22). And as that dwelling place, it's our job to carry his message to the world, so that "through the church, the manifold wisdom of God should be made known to the rulers and authorities in the heavenly realms, according to his eternal purpose that he accomplished in Christ Jesus our Lord" (3:10–11). What's more, Paul recognized that as the church proclaimed the wisdom of God to the world and to the rulers and authorities in the heavenly realms, they would face opposition. So, he warned the people of God to "take [a] stand against the devil's schemes" and to prepare for a fight (6:11–12). In Ephesians 6:13–17 he wrote,

> Therefore put on the full armor of God, so that when the day of evil comes, you may be able to stand your ground, and after you have done everything, to stand. Stand firm then, with the belt of truth

buckled around your waist, with the breastplate of righteousness in place, and with your feet fitted with the readiness that comes from the gospel of peace. In addition to all this, take up the shield of faith, with which you can extinguish all the flaming arrows of the evil one. Take the helmet of salvation and the sword of the Spirit, which is the word of God.

That passage begs a question, doesn't it? If our message was meant to stay cooped up in the walls of a building, who would need armor?

As we've explored throughout this book, the world around us is falling under the influence of the evil one. America has given itself to his delusions and has found itself mired in violence and chaos. It lacks peace. It's swimming in a cesspool of sexual desire. Yes, it is a virtual hell on earth here in America, but there's good news: Jesus came to save America from its wickedness, and he's chosen us, the church, to be the vehicle for that message. He's chosen us to be his very presence in the world, to push back the darkness around us with the light of his love.

American church, listen up: We are a collection of mobile homes for the Almighty. We carry his truth wherever we go. If you're a member of the church, it's time to stop hiding in the safety of your worship services. It's time to go out into the world and be the church, to live its mission out loud.

In the voting booth.

In the public schools.

In the workplace.

Wherever you are, you are the church, a vehicle for the good news of Jesus.

★　★　★

Lord, I'm ready to start living my faith out loud, on mission for you. Show me where you want me to go into the world and be the church, expressing my worship as I go.

DAY 69 ★ TAKE THE GOSPEL
TO THE WORLD

**Always be prepared to give an answer to
everyone who asks you to give the reason
for the hope that you have. But do this
with gentleness and respect.**
—1 PETER 3:15

I couldn't say how many folks have dropped in on Miss Kay and me over the years. No matter how they come, Miss Kay and I welcome them in, and I give them a double-barrel helping of the truth.

I remember the time a young redneck, his girlfriend, mother, and a dozen of their friends came knocking a few years back. As they sat in our living room, it became apparent that the young man and his lady were shacking up. I looked at the boy and asked him straight.

"Y'all aren't married, are you?"

"No," he said.

"And let me guess: you've been getting into her britches, haven't you?"

His face turned red, and he nodded.

"The Bible calls that sin," I said, "but let me tell you the good news of the One who can forgive all your sins, raise you to new life, and solve your biggest problem—death."

The boy and his girlfriend listened to my gospel presentation, and like so many others, they were taken with it. After I'd finished my spiel, I asked whether they wanted to move on the message, and they all but ran out the door toward the river. Just below my house, while the boy's mama and his group of friends watched, I lowered the two into the waters of baptism. As I raised the boy out of the water, I told him he was a new creature.

"This means you can't go back to shacking up with that pretty young girl till you're married," I said. "Understand?"

He smiled, then made a beeline to his girlfriend. There, on the banks of the Ouachita, he dropped to one knee and asked her to marry him.

"I can make a phone call and get a wedding license," I said. "We can make it official right here."

He agreed, and his mama was beaming from ear to ear.

This is just one example of what can happen when we offer ourselves as sacrifices of worship to the Almighty. He'll use us to bring the good news of Jesus to a world stuck in its own sin. He'll use us to bring freedom and peace of mind. He'll use us to change America, person by person, life by life, soul by soul. And as that happens, the very soul of America will be transformed.

Christ is the hope for a lost world, a world that will never darken the doors of the church. And if enough of us take our mission seriously, if we refuse to believe the lie that we should keep our faith confined to a two-hour church service, we might make a dent in this godless country. We might change the hearts of Americans and convince them of the other truths of Scripture. In short, we might keep America from becoming a living hell on earth.

So, here's the call, American church, and it's the same call Christ gave us on the mountain: get out of your structures; go into the world; carry the good news of Jesus as you go; preach the message in the voting booth, in the public schools, at your workplace; offer your homes, your hospitality, your homemade soup and corn bread to your unbelieving neighbors; make disciples; baptize; bring freedom to those who'll never darken the doors of the church. This is your very act of worship. This is what it means to be the church, Christ's presence to a dying world.

★　　★　　★

Lord, thank you for sending someone to tell me the good news and show me the way to you, or else I would still be lost. Help me to be ready to share that good news with others as it was shared with me.

DAY 70 ★ ALL THE SCRIPTURES POINT TO A KING

The LORD has established his throne in heaven,
and his kingdom rules over all.
—PSALM 103:19

As I studied the Bible, I began to notice something curious. From Genesis to Revelation, I saw a theme threading through. Time and time again, the Scriptures spoke of God the Almighty, the King of kings and Lord of lords. He was the sovereign ruler, and he made no bones about it.

I noticed the kingly thread in Exodus. There, Moses led the Israelites away from the tyrant king of Egypt and toward the promised land. As they marched from Egypt and toward the land God would give them, they worshipped and sang, "The LORD reigns for ever and ever" (15:18). On that long journey to the promised land, the Almighty called to Moses from a mountaintop. There, he told Moses he was establishing "a kingdom of priests and a holy nation" (19:6). Who reigned over that kingdom? The Lord, the one who was leading them home. Only one chapter later, the Almighty laid down the law of that kingdom, giving Moses the Ten Commandments.

In Deuteronomy, the sovereign theme appeared again. There, Moses reminded the people of the laws handed down from the mountain. He called the people to live by those laws of God, the God whom Moses called the "God of gods and Lord of lords, the great God, mighty and awesome, who shows no partiality and accepts no bribes" (10:17). *Lord*. What is that if not a term of kingship?

In Daniel, an earthly king fell on his face and recognized that his sovereignty was no match for that of the Almighty. The evil ruler Nebuchadnezzar of Babylon, the king who'd persecuted God's chosen people, fell before the Almighty's prophet and declared, "Surely your God is the God of gods and the Lord of kings" (2:47). Nebuchadnezzar, the most powerful king of his age, recognized that there was an authority greater than his own.

I flipped to Psalms and found still more kingly references. The psalmist wrote, "The LORD has established his throne in heaven, and his kingdom rules over all" (103:19). He'd been the king forever, the one who ruled over the wandering Israelites, over Nebuchadnezzar, and over my little plot of land on the Ouachita River.

I discovered that the prophets spoke of the King, too, and they recognized the King demands holiness. Consider Isaiah. After his vision of the Almighty, he cried out, "I am ruined! For I am a man of unclean lips, and I live among a people of unclean lips, and my eyes have seen the King, the LORD Almighty" (Isa. 6:5). In his presence, Isaiah confessed just how unholy he was. In the presence of the King, Isaiah repented.

The sovereign thread ran through the Old Testament, but it didn't stop there. It carried through into the New Testament, the testament of the King who came from heaven to earth.

★　　★　　★

Lord, I am like Isaiah, a man of unclean lips among an unclean people. I worship you as the King of all the earth, the sovereign ruler of the universe. You alone are worthy of worship and praise.

DAY 71 ★ FOLLOWING KING JESUS

The kingdom of God is in your midst.
—LUKE 17:21

Throughout his ministry, Jesus didn't mince words about his kingship. When Jesus met Nathanael, when he told the would-be disciple where he'd been just the hour before, Nathanael declared, "You are the king of Israel" (John 1:49).

In the gospel of Luke, the Pharisees asked Jesus when God's kingdom would come. Jesus gave it to them straight: "The kingdom of God is in your midst" (17:21).

In the gospel of Matthew, Jesus sent his disciples into the countryside. He gave them simple instructions:

> Do not go among the Gentiles or enter any town of the Samaritans. Go rather to the lost sheep of Israel. As you go, proclaim this message: "The kingdom of heaven has come near." (10:5–7)

In the gospel of Mark, Jesus shared about his coming suffering and death. He taught, "Whoever wants to be my disciple must deny themselves and take up their cross and follow me" (8:34). But then he offered his followers the most astounding promise: "Truly I tell you, some who are standing here will not taste death before they see that the kingdom of God has come with power" (9:1). See his words? The kingdom would come with power before the disciples died. Why? Because he, the King, had come to bring the kingdom. It was a bold statement, one that locked down the time line. The kingdom was already on earth, right in their midst.

Even in Jesus' last hours, Pontius Pilate asked him, "'Are you the king of the Jews?' Jesus answered, 'You have said so.'" (Mark 15:2). These were the last words Jesus said before being handed over to the guards. And what did the guards do?

They put a purple robe on him, then twisted together a crown of thorns and set it on him. And they began to call out to him, "Hail, king of the Jews!" (vv. 17–18)

The guards didn't know they were murdering the King of the universe. Still, Mark recorded their words as an affirmation of the truth.

After Jesus' death, resurrection, and ascension, his people continued to follow King Jesus, continued to carry his message into the world. During Paul's ministry, he visited the Gentile churches, "preaching the kingdom" (Acts 20:25). While under Roman guard, Paul held a revival, "explaining about the kingdom of God" to the Jews living in Rome (Acts 28:23). He stayed under house arrest in Rome for two years, and while he was there, "he proclaimed the kingdom of God and taught about the Lord Jesus Christ—with all boldness and without hindrance" (Acts 28:31). He wrote letters to his protégé, Timothy, in which he offered these closing lines: "Now to the King eternal, immortal, invisible, the only God, be honor and glory for ever and ever. Amen" (1 Tim. 1:17).

To put an exclamation point on it all, the Spirit of God visited the apostle John while he was exiled on the island of Patmos for his belief in King Jesus. During that visitation, John was given a vision of King Jesus:

I saw heaven standing open and there before me was a white horse, whose rider is called Faithful and True. With justice he judges and wages war. His eyes are like blazing fire, and on his head are many crowns. . . . On his robe and on his thigh he has this name written:

KING OF KINGS AND LORD OF LORDS. (Rev. 19:11–12, 16)

★　　★　　★

King Jesus, I praise you as King of the universe. I will follow you as my King and boldly proclaim the message of your kingdom on earth until you return someday to rule in righteousness forever.

DAY 72 ★ PROCLAIM THE TRUTH

How, then, can they call on the one they have not
believed in? And how can they believe in the one
of whom they have not heard? And how can they
hear without someone preaching to them?
—ROMANS 10:14

I was sitting in my living room—our home served as the Duck
Commander office back in those days—when the phone rang.

"Hello. Duck Commander. This is Phil."

"I need to order some duck calls," the man on the other end of
the phone said.

I asked him what he'd like, and he started in on his order. He
started listing calls, and for whatever reason, he used the Lord's name
in vain. Twice. Three times. The fourth time he used Jesus' name, I
knew what I had to do.

"Let me ask you something," I said after I'd written down his
MasterCard number. "Why would you curse the only One who could
save you from eternal death?"

There was silence on the other end of the line.

"You still there?"

He responded flatly, "Yeah, I'm still here, Hoss. You got my duck
call order?"

"Yeah. I got it," I said.

The receiver slammed down on the other side.

Ten minutes passed, and the phone rang again.

"Hello. Duck Commander. This is Phil."

"It's me again," the familiar voice said.

"Well, what about it?" I said. "Why would you curse the only One
who could save you from death?"

He said, "I've never really thought about it."

"Well, you're going six feet deep one of these days," I said, "and you cannot escape it without divine intervention." I looked up the contact information from his order sheet and said, "You ought to drive over to West Monroe and let me tell you a story. When I'm finished, I bet you won't curse God anymore."

I reckon he took it as some sort of challenge, because he said, "Well, I might do that, Hoss!"

A week went by, and I was sitting in my recliner when I heard a knock at the door. I told whomever it was to come on in, and a fella stepped into my living room, buddy in tow.

"I'm that fella who was cursing God on the phone, and I ain't leaving until you tell me why I shouldn't."

"Well, friend, you have come to the right place," I said.

There in my living room, I told the gentlemen the good news of Jesus. I finished, then asked whether they'd like to go down to the river to be baptized. They said they'd like to move on the good news before they made their way back to Decatur. So I took them down to the river and baptized them.

Seventeen years later, I was in Decatur, Alabama, to preach at a local church. When I was eating dinner with the preacher, one of the brothers at the table asked if I remembered so-and-so. "He was the ol' boy who'd cursed God while ordering some duck calls and you challenged him over it."

"Oh, yes. I remember," I said.

"He came home after that meeting at your place, and he gave it to us real good for never sharing the gospel with him. He told us he shouldn't have had to drive all the way to Louisiana to find a man who'd challenge him on his sin and lead him into the truth."

"Whatever happened to him?" I asked.

"He's one of the leaders of this church now."

The man who'd used his freedom of speech to curse the Almighty now used it to preach his name, I was told.

There is power in the gospel when it's preached. It sets people free. It changes folks' lives. It puts us on the path to everlasting life. But how in the world will people come to know this freedom if there aren't any preachers? And how can there be preachers if folks don't exercise their God-given and constitutionally recognized freedom of speech?

Lord, thank you for your saving power to transform lives for your kingdom. Give me the boldness and the words to exercise my freedom of speech to proclaim your good news to others.

DAY 73 ★ PREACHING WITH ZEAL

**Never be lacking in zeal, but keep your
spiritual fervor, serving the Lord.**
—ROMANS 12:11

What should we do with this great truth of truths, the truth of the Almighty's love? We should put our faith in it and organize our whole lives around it. As Paul wrote to the Ephesians, we should "follow God's example, therefore, as dearly loved children and walk in the way of love, just as Christ loved us and gave himself up for us as a fragrant offering and sacrifice to God" (5:1–2). But merely believing the truth isn't enough. We also stake our lives on it. We preach, preach, preach, in duck season and out of duck season (my paraphrase of 2 Timothy 4:2). Every day. All day. Unapologetically. We must preach the news of God's love in our public schools, our public squares, and our voting booths. We speak of the Almighty's saving power—to the teachers and principals, the mayors and governors, or in my case, President Trump himself. We remind the world that Jesus has made a way for them to conquer misery, disease, and death. In eternity? Yes. But here too.

Why do we preach the truth so relentlessly? Because we love our neighbors as much as we love ourselves.

I suppose some who are under the delusions of the evil one will read this book, challenge my love for them, and maybe even accuse me of hate speech for calling out their sin. I suspect they'll call me a crazy old graybeard for preaching the truth in these pages the only way I know how. They can say whatever they like, because the truth is, I've given my life to this message, and I only know one way to preach it—*with great zeal*. "Zeal?" you ask. That's right. Zeal. That's how Paul taught us to preach when he wrote to the Romans, "Never be lacking in zeal, but keep your spiritual fervor, serving the Lord"

(12:11). What is zeal? *Merriam-Webster* defines it as "intense heat." It's the boiling point. So when folks see my passion for the things of God, when they call me a Bible banger or a zealot, when they mock me for preaching the good news, they're simply recognizing the heat. That ain't a bad thing.

I've adopted an open-carry policy when it comes to my zeal for God. It's that open-carry policy that's made me a target in the media, this much is true. They've held my faith under the microscope of public scrutiny, but they haven't caught me in any scandal. They haven't caught me drinking or doing drugs or running around on Miss Kay. Instead, they've only found one thing—an unwavering commitment to the absolute truth of who Jesus is and how his love can change a life.

Lord, give me a passion for the things of you. Help me to not shy away from opportunities to share the gospel but instead boldly proclaim your message of salvation and live out my faith with great zeal in the public square.

DAY 74 ★ WHEN DOING GOOD MEANS REVOLUTION

So do not be ashamed of the testimony about our Lord or of me his prisoner. Rather, join with me in suffering for the gospel, by the power of God.
—2 TIMOTHY 1:8

King Jesus himself showed how true kingdom living sometimes involves some form of action.

Jesus, the man who did good in every way, refused to follow the unjust and ungodly laws and rules of his own society from time to time. In his day, a group of religious lawyers brought a woman to him who'd been caught in adultery, the legal penalty for which was public execution by stoning. Did Jesus uphold the unjust law and terminate the woman's life? Nope. Instead, he showed mercy, turning the law around on those trying to enforce it. To the men holding rocks, he said, "Let any one of you who is without sin be the first to throw a stone at her" (John 8:7). The men, of course, turned tail and walked away.

Sometimes words were not enough, though. Just before his unjust crucifixion, Jesus entered Jerusalem to celebrate the Passover. There he saw the moneychangers in the temple swindling the people by selling impure animals, a practice that was perfectly legal. He turned the tables over and drove the merchants out, telling them not to dirty the house of the Almighty (Mark 11:15–17). He rebelled against the order of the day, likely breaking a law or two in the process. And why? Because he believed protecting the house of the King was more important than going along with the immoral, godless, swindling behavior of the religious leaders of the day.

Consider the thousands of Bible-believing pastors in America who may one day have to choose between honoring God's definition of the family or performing same-sex weddings. Consider a day when speaking out about Christian beliefs might be labeled a federal offense.

Yes, kingdom living requires us to do good so long as we have the freedom to pursue it. But it requires us to stand firm in our faith, too, even if it means being mocked by the media, having our businesses shut down, or even being imprisoned. It means fighting for the right to live a godly life and never capitulating to the evil one.

So as you consider what it means to live a kingdom-oriented life, as you consider how to advance what's godly and how to fight against what's evil, ask yourself:

- Do I strive to live a good and godly life? Do I take my kingdom living to the streets?
- Do I speak out and act against unjust or ungodly laws, laws that would require me to disobey the King?

Do your part for the kingdom by doing good, by living godly lives that influence the world around you. Invite folks to your table, share your resources, speak out against godless tyranny, then share the good news of King Jesus with everyone. Who knows, maybe one or two will join you in this journey of kingdom living. And if enough of us bring just one or two new people into this way of Jesus Politics, we might become a political force to be reckoned with. We might become a mighty throng ready to win back the soul of America.

Lord, when I look around, I see the chaos, fear, and division in our land. Help me to take action to do my part for the kingdom by showing your love and truth to others.

DAY 75 ★ THE KINGDOM IN ACTION

If any of you lacks wisdom, you should ask God, who gives generously to all without finding fault, and it will be given to you.
—JAMES 1:5

If Jesus were to come down from on high to speak directly to our country's politics today, I believe he'd urge us to speak out and act on our faith. He'd encourage us to

- Elect politicians who refuse to pass ordinances and laws requiring citizens of the kingdom to compromise on their values
- Elect godly men and women who will pass laws that protect our religious liberties, our freedom to call sin what it is, and our freedom to invite your neighbors into the kingdom of God
- Elect those who will vet all judges and confirm only those who honor and uphold the godly heritage of our country
- Elect judges who will uphold the constitutional rights of the people and strike down any laws that infringe on our religious liberties
- Empower those who are morally upright, who demonstrate allegiance to King Jesus in the way they speak, act, and treat others

I can see the question turning over in your mind, especially as it relates to the last item.

What if no godly men or women are running, Phil? What if neither politician in any given race is morally upright?

In that case, I suppose we ought to vote for those politicians who'll protect our rights to express our faith, regardless of their own behavior.

Men and women who might be works in progress from a biblical perspective, but who wouldn't enact laws or confirm judges who'd shut
down the citizens of the King.

So as you go into the voting booth, whether in the next election
cycle or any other, ask yourself these questions:

- Which candidate will protect my right to express my religious
  beliefs in the public square?
- Which candidate will protect my right to express my religious
  beliefs in my private business?
- Which candidate will appoint judges who understand the
  importance of religious liberty, who will help us return to the
  sure foundation of God's Word?
- Which candidate will stand up to the atheists who would
  build a country on a plywood foundation?

And once you've come to a godly conclusion, do your duty. Act
on the King's manifesto and do your part to rebuild the foundation of
America on godly principles.

★ ★ ★

*Lord, you are the source of wisdom and understanding. Help me to be wise
in the candidates I support and not deceived by smooth words and slick
presentations. May I keep my eyes on you alone and trust in your truth.*

DAY 76 ★ GOD'S PRECISE CREATION

He set the earth on its foundations;
   it can never be moved.
—PSALM 104:5

In the beginning God created the heavens and the earth. Then the King made the sun, and the earth orbited around it. But the foundations of the earth—the North and South Poles—were not set to be equal distances away from the sun. Instead, the earth's axis was tilted ever so slightly. And as I've come to understand it, it's this tilt that's set the conditions for creation to flourish.

The earth's axial tilt is slight, sitting at precisely 23.5 degrees. And this tilt accounts for the earth's weather and the changing seasons. Because of this tilt, there are times in the earth's orbit when West Monroe is closer to the sun. This accounts for our sweltering summers. As the earth moves around the sun, as it reaches the opposite side of the orbit, the same 23.5-degree tilt ensures West Monroe is just a little bit farther from the sun. This brings winter's edge, and with it the migration of the ducks I love to harvest.[1] But what if the earth were tilted a few degrees one way or the other? Well, life as we know it might not exist on Planet Earth.

It's not just the tilt of the earth's axis that makes our planet inhabitable. We've been given water, which comes in handy around duck-hunting season. Our earth is the perfect distance from the sun, which makes plant and animal life possible. The Almighty has set the conditions for an inhabitable world. And what the Creator set in motion, his creation cannot stop. We cannot knock the world off its axis, can't shake it from its foundations. So what kind of arrogance possesses us to think we could destroy the thing God so precisely made for us?

God created a precise ecosystem for us and all his creation. This being the case, we ought to ask ourselves why.

In the beginning, God created a garden and put man and woman smack in the middle of it. Our charge was simple: work the earth and take care of it (Gen. 2:15). The Almighty gave us dominion over the earth, made us to "rule over the fish in the sea and the birds in the sky, over the livestock and all the wild animals, and over all the creatures that move along the ground" (1:26). Then the Almighty gave us "every seed-bearing plant on the face of the whole earth and every tree that has fruit with seed in it" (v. 29) as a food supply.

After the great flood in Noah's day, the Almighty said, "Everything that lives and moves about will be food for you. Just as I gave you the green plants, I now give you everything" (Gen. 9:3). With that verse, we got new orders from headquarters: meat is in. If it walks, crawls, flies, or swims, we can whack it and stack it. Skin it and fin it. Grill it. Roast it. Deep fat fry it. Eat it up.

Yes, the Almighty made us stewards of the earth. He gave us freedom to cultivate it and eat from it. He gave us freedom to hunt the animals too. And he did all of it for our enjoyment. He did it so we'd remember his goodness.

★   ★   ★

God, thank you for your marvelous creation that you designed precisely to nourish us and sustain us. Help me to be a good steward of the earth—cultivating it, eating from it, and enjoying it.

DAY 77 ★ THE AUTHOR OF ALL LIFE

This is the account of the heavens and the earth when they were created, when the Lord God made the earth and the heavens.
—GENESIS 2:4

God is the Author of all life—human, animal, plant. And as if to remove any question, the entire Bible starts with this sentence: "In the beginning God created the heavens and the earth" (Gen. 1:1). But he didn't just create life. He also organized it all for the benefit of his greatest creation: mankind. The Genesis account seems to make this plain too. After making a beautiful garden, God placed man and woman in it and then gave them a simple task: be fruitful, multiply, and fill the earth. But how would man get what he needed to be fruitful and multiply? How would his needs be met? God thought that through. All that other life the Almighty had created? He'd allow men to use it to sustain their own lives. The writer of Genesis recorded it this way:

> Then God said, "Let Us make man in Our image, according to Our likeness; let them have dominion over the fish of the sea, over the birds of the air, and over the cattle, over all the earth and over every creeping thing that creeps on the earth." (Gen. 1:26 NKJV)

Just chapters later, after God brought Noah and his family through the flood, he gave a similar command to Noah:

> Be fruitful and increase in number and fill the earth. The fear and dread of you will fall on all the beasts of the earth, and on all the birds in the sky, on every creature that moves along the ground, and on all the fish in the sea; they are given into your hands. Everything that lives and moves about will be food for you. Just as I gave you the green plants, I now give you everything. (9:1–3)

God gave us everything we needed to sustain our lives. Plant life for wood and construction materials, animal life for food and fur—God allows us to use those things for our benefit.

The question remains: What is the purpose of all this life the Almighty created for us? Why did he give us plants and animals to subdue for our own provision? The answer is simple: God wanted us to understand his goodness (Acts 17:25, 27).

God wanted us to see the ways he created life to feed us, nourish us, and help us flourish, and through that, he wanted us to know just how much he loves us. He left us a game trail straight to his character. As Paul would later write to the Romans, God wanted his love for us to be "understood from what has been made, so that people are without excuse" (1:20).

It's pretty simple, really. God, the Author of life, created the perfect conditions to sustain man. He gave us plants to cultivate, to use for food and shelter. He gave us animals to harvest for food and clothing. The Author of life had a pretty good plan: create life to sustain life. And when we remember nature's purpose, when we remember the truth of its sustaining force, it should always and ever point us back to the goodness of the Almighty. It should remind us of how much he cares for and loves us.

★　　★　　★

God, thank you for your creation, which reveals to us your goodness. Every time I look outside at the wonders of your creation, may I worship you as the Author of all life.

DAY 78 ★ THE PURPOSE OF THE ENVIRONMENT

For since the creation of the world God's invisible
qualities—his eternal power and divine nature—have
been clearly seen, being understood from what has
been made, so that people are without excuse.
—ROMANS 1:20

The Scriptures are clear about the purpose of the environment. In the book of Hebrews, the writer begins a run on faith with a statement about creation: "By faith we understand that the universe was formed at God's command, so that what is seen was not made out of what was visible" (11:3). In the book of Romans, Paul wrote: "For since the creation of the world God's invisible qualities—his eternal power and divine nature—have been clearly seen, being understood from what has been made, so that people are without excuse" (1:20). See? Everything in creation was meant to point us to the Creator.

Everything? you ask.

Everything, I say.

Cucumbers, tomatoes, and onions?

Mix 'em in a salad bowl and tell me they aren't the work of the Almighty.

Mallards and teal?

You ever eat a duck gumbo, dude?

What about oil or petroleum?

Consider how God created gasoline for our cars, how he allows us to use it for transportation. Consider how gasoline has been used to spread the gospel.

King Jesus knew the purpose of creation better than any of us, knew how it could be used as a point of connection with the Almighty.

Jesus himself took to nature to hear from God. On more than one occasion he withdrew to the wilderness, the desert, or a mountain to connect with his Father in prayer. He used nature as a teaching tool too. In the Sermon on the Mount, he pointed to the birds and the flowers, told us not to worry about what we'd eat or wear because we'd be fed and clothed better than fowls and flora (Matt. 6:25–29). In the parable of the sower, he used creation to show how the kingdom of God grows:

> As he was scattering the seed, some fell along the path, and the birds came and ate it up. Some fell on rocky places, where it did not have much soil. It sprang up quickly, because the soil was shallow. But when the sun came up, the plants were scorched, and they withered because they had no root. Other seed fell among thorns, which grew up and choked the plants. Still other seed fell on good soil, where it produced a crop—a hundred, sixty or thirty times what was sown. Whoever has ears, let them hear. (Matt. 13:4–9)

Jesus, the Word of creation incarnate, used the natural world to point us to the King.

★　　★　　★

God, everything in creation points us to you, the Creator. Whenever I'm tempted to be anxious, help me to remember that you take care of the birds and flowers—and you will also take care of me.

DAY 79 ★ FROM LAWLESS LIBERAL TO NEW LIFE

The Word became flesh and made his dwelling among
us. We have seen his glory, the glory of the one and only
Son, who came from the Father, full of grace and truth.
—JOHN 1:14

Robert (not his real name) was a media type, a city slicker who'd been a self-described leftist. In his years in the media, he'd run around with powerful politicians, and he knew many of the movers and shakers on the Left. Legislated gay marriage, legalized abortion, the environmental movement, stripping God from the public square—he was all for it. But somehow he'd found himself at a conservative political rally, and I was the featured speaker.

I'd stepped onto the stage and shared the good news of King Jesus. He'd come from heaven to earth with a particular intention, I said. Salvation of the souls of men. It was a statement Robert had never heard before, and as he listened, he was moved by the most shocking statement. It was so shocking, in fact, that he wrote it down.

"Mankind could not get our hands on God to harm him unless he became a human. So that's what God did. Ultimately, he was murdered by mankind, rose again, and that's how he saved the world."

Robert wrote me a letter about how he began shaking all over when he heard these words, how he was crushed by the realization that if God came into the world today, Robert would be among the crucifiers. It was the moment he knew he had to learn more about this King of the universe who subjected himself to the lawless acts of men so he could save the world. He left the rally that night and began studying. He started reading the Bible verses I cited in the show, which led him to other passages about King Jesus. And as he read, he believed.

His letter concluded by asking if he could visit Miss Kay and me on the river, and he left me his contact information. I quickly invited him.

A few weeks later, Robert sat in my living room and retold his story. He recounted his convictions, how he'd previously believed we should keep God out of government, how he supported using the law to advance godless policies. But when he heard of a God who had become human, everything changed for him, and he knew he had to follow this King. That decision had led him on a journey, and that journey had landed him on my couch.

We spent three hours together, talking through the truth of the gospel. When our conversation drew to a close, I asked, "You been baptized yet?"

"Not yet," he said.

"You want to?"

"Let's do it."

And with that, Robert followed me out the front door and down to the receding waters of the Ouachita River, and I baptized him right there in the river in the name of the Father, Son, and the Holy Spirit.

Robert came out of the water a new man that day. He changed his clothes, ate a bite, then drove away from the Robertson camp happy, happy, happy. I've kept up with his progress. He's been true to his word and the Word of the Almighty. He's left the lawless ways of living behind and has signed on with the King. He's sharing his new life with the world around him (I hope he's shared extra with his liberal cronies), and as he has, the kingdom—the kingdom whose law is love—keeps moving forward.

★ ★ ★

God, help me to remember that no one is too far for you to reach with your gospel. Help me to take action to share your good news even with those who are lawless and far from you, knowing that you can turn their hearts as your kingdom keeps moving forward.

DAY 80 ★ YOUR MARCHING ORDERS

Therefore go and make disciples of all nations,
baptizing them in the name of the Father and of the
Son and of the Holy Spirit, and teaching them to
obey everything I have commanded you. And surely
I am with you always, to the very end of the age.
—MATTHEW 28:19–20

M y story isn't a testament to me. It's a testament to the saving power of a living and loving God. It's the story of how the truth of Jesus can change one man, how it can spread through one man to feed thousands—friends, business acquaintances, customers, and television viewers alike. My story is just one example of how the truth of the gospel can change the masses, truth by truth, person by person. And if enough of us begin to live into this transformative truth of God's love, if we combat the lies of the enemy with the truth of Scriptures, if we preach the truth in the darkest places—just like Bill Smith did—what might happen here in America? My guess is we'd see God's saving power take hold of this country. We'd see people turn back to God. If enough folks turned and gave their lives to the Almighty, I believe we'd see a country committed to God once again. We'd find ourselves with virtuous leaders, leaders courageous enough to enact godly laws and stand against evils like abortion and the changing definitions of marriage. We'd return to civility, to the brotherly love that trumps division and hate. Through the power of the Almighty, we'd become a more unified people.

Pay attention to the marching orders Jesus left us:

> Therefore go and make disciples of all nations, baptizing them in the name of the Father and of the Son and of the Holy Spirit, and teaching them to obey everything I have commanded you. And surely I am with you always, to the very end of the age. (Matt. 28:19–20)

Rest assured: until I take my last breath, I aim to carry out these orders. Join me in the mission of proclaiming the truth of God's love to an America who's been sold a bill of goods, a country who is intent on kill'n God. And as you go into the darkest places to preach that truth, know this: Jesus is with you as you go, all the way to the end.

King Jesus, I want to follow you and proclaim the truth. Help me to fulfill my marching orders for your kingdom, going into the world and proclaiming to all the good news of your salvation until you take me home.

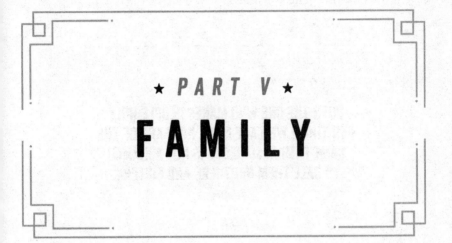

★ *PART V* ★

FAMILY

BOTH THE ONE WHO MAKES PEOPLE HOLY
AND THOSE WHO ARE MADE HOLY ARE OF THE
SAME FAMILY. SO JESUS IS NOT ASHAMED
TO CALL THEM BROTHERS AND SISTERS.

—HEBREWS 2:11

DAY 81 ★ CHASING FREEDOM

You, my brothers and sisters, were called to be free.
But do not use your freedom to indulge the flesh;
rather, serve one another humbly in love.
—GALATIANS 5:13

I watched Miss Kay's Volkswagen Bug pull from the trailer and disappear. She'd taken whatever household items she could—some kitchen utensils, a few pots and pans, three folding lawn chairs, the black-and-white television—and stuffed them into the trunk. She'd loaded the boys into their seats and crammed their clothes and keepsakes around them. She'd even taken their toothbrushes.

Miss Kay, my wife of only a few years, was leaving. Maybe for good.

Before the fight that resulted in me showing Miss Kay the door, I'd been at home alone with the boys: Alan, Jason, and Willie. I was sitting on the porch, fuming while I waited to go out with my friends per my usual routine. As I sat and stewed, and the seconds ticked by, I grew more restless. I'd already started drinking and was about half-lit when Miss Kay finally walked through the front door.

"You're late," I said. "Again."

She apologized and blamed it on work, but I thought I knew better, and I told her so. I accused her of running around on me. I accused her of lying to cover it up. I was sure she was a cheater, I said, and though there was no real evidence to bolster my accusation, I was convinced. And what was most upsetting, her running around had disrupted my night. It had interfered with my plans for freedom and fun, my fishing, drinking, and carousing in the woods on State Line Road. This was the last time.

The argument escalated. So did my voice. And that's when I said the words that triggered a series of life-altering events, the words that would eventually open the door of God's grace to me.

"You're ruining my life!" I roared.

"You've been ruining my life for ten years!" she yelled back.

"Get out," I said, pointing to the door, "and take your kids with you!" As if they weren't my kids too.

Miss Kay shook from head to toe while she gathered what she could as fast as she could. Still, she knew this was the end of the line. She didn't grovel. She didn't beg. She was resolved to give me exactly what I'd asked for. In less than an hour she'd disappeared into a Louisiana rainstorm. I stood in that rain and watched her go, and there, in that moment, I had no remorse. I thought I'd fixed my problem. I thought I was finally free.

Of course, a fight of this magnitude isn't made in a moment or a day or even a month. This last standoff between Miss Kay and me grew from years of unrest. What was the source of that unrest? I suppose I thought Miss Kay was cramping my style. I needed freedom, and for so many years, I'd been busy chasing some version of it. Freedom from the structure. Freedom from the law. Freedom from the rules.

God, I know that nothing in this world—no person, experience, or politics—can make me truly free. Thank you for sending your Son to die in my place so I can experience the real freedom of salvation.

DAY 82 ★ PRAYING FOR RECONCILIATION

If any [husbands] do not believe the word, they may be won over without words by the behavior of their wives, when they see the purity and reverence of your lives.
—1 PETER 3:1–2

I'd been reared by a God-fearing mother and father, and for as long as I can remember, they had me in church. I attended my fair share of Sunday morning services at my country Church of Christ, heard sermon after sermon for eighteen years. I took Communion, drank the grape juice, and ate the stale crackers. I heard message after message about what it meant to be a member of the church. "Hear, believe, repent, confess, and be baptized," they said, but what any of it meant was beyond me. It was religious talk, mumbo jumbo. All I knew for sure was that I was supposed to follow the rules—don't drink; don't cuss; don't dance. I was supposed to behave like the church folks, even if behaving wasn't my strong suit. And it wasn't.

I didn't have the benefit of the Scriptures in those days. No one had taught me the plain truth: God was not dead. He was alive, and he'd written his law, the law of right and wrong, on my heart. I didn't know that my guilt was a result of violating the very real law of a very real and living God.

If I had known the truth, maybe I would have understood why my conscience ached and why I felt so isolated and alone. But I didn't. And so even with Miss Kay and the kids gone, even in the absence of responsibility, even in my bachelor's paradise, I couldn't escape my misery. Hunting, fishing, and partying had all lost their luster. I was ten times more a prisoner after Miss Kay left, and I knew it within the first week.

Little did I know, Miss Kay had her own encounter with the living God. She'd always believed in him, but after she left me, she went all in. She'd given everything in her life to him, and somewhere, miles away from my trailer prison, she was praying. She was praying I'd be miserable in my sin. She was praying that misery would drive me into the arms of God. She was praying that God would reconcile our marriage, our family. Miss Kay was praying for my freedom.

I think it was the power of those prayers that wouldn't let me wallow in my misery for more than a month. And when that misery became too much to bear, and when I came to understand how empty my life was, I slid into the driver's seat of my truck and I set off to find Miss Kay.

I cried from the minute I hit the city limits to the time I pulled into the store parking lot. I bawled, in fact—a thing I'd been too proud to do for most of my life. In that parking lot I sat in my truck, engine idling, head on my steering wheel, wondering what I'd say to Miss Kay. But before I could get up the nerve to open the truck door, there she was, tapping on my window. I rolled it down.

She didn't say anything at first. She just stood there, staring. I broke the silence.

"I'm miserable," I told her. "I just want my family back."

God, thank you that you offer us so much more than rules—you give us a satisfying relationship with you. Help me to pray for my loved ones to experience a saving relationship with you.

DAY 83 ★ GOD PROVIDES FOR HIS CHILDREN

The LORD does not let the righteous go hungry,
but he thwarts the craving of the wicked.
—PROVERBS 10:3

I found the profession of teaching to be very kind to me in those early years of faith. It was a good job, and it gave Miss Kay and the boys the financial stability they needed. It allowed me to influence and pour into the young men of Northern Louisiana, too, and that felt good. But even as my students and the administrators grew more and more comfortable with having a country boy with a master's degree in the classroom, I was growing more uncomfortable. I felt the pull of God's creation, the call of the river. (You can take a rat out of the river, but I don't suppose you can ever take the river out of the rat.) I felt the tug of business, and the business I wanted more than anything was to make duck calls.

Was it a crazy idea? Probably.

Would God provide? I figured he would.

How'd I know? I believed the truth of God's Word.

In my time devouring the Scriptures, I'd read that God provides for his children. I took God's promise in the Proverbs to heart, how he'd never let his children go hungry (10:3). I read the Psalms and noted his promise to satisfy the thirsty and give good food to his children (107:9). I read the writings of Paul and believed what he told the Philippians, namely, "God will meet all your needs according to the riches of his glory in Christ Jesus" (4:19). I read and read and read, and I started practicing the teachings of the Scriptures. As I saw their fruit in my life, I came to the conclusion that the truth of the Scriptures was absolute. And if this was so, I knew I had to go all in: I had to believe either all of it or none of it. And so, with little more than a three-year-old faith and a blind trust in the truth of God's Word, I set to planning.

I examined our finances—the savings we had put away for a rainy day—and considered what I could bring in as a commercial fisherman on the river. By my calculations, between my savings and what I could make fishing the Ouachita, we had a three-year window for me to try and get a duck call business off the ground. That was enough for me. I knew God would come through and that he'd take care of Miss Kay and me if this dream was from him. But how would I convince Miss Kay?

Come to find out, it was easier than I thought it'd be. I told her the scheme and she agreed. That's all it took. We were off to the races.

Lord, thank you for your promise to provide for my needs. Show me your way, and strengthen me to walk obediently into the future, leading my family with confidence in you.

DAY 84 ★ TEACHING CHILDREN ABOUT GOD

These commandments that I give you today are to be on your hearts. Impress them on your children. Talk about them when you sit at home and when you walk along the road, when you lie down and when you get up.
—DEUTERONOMY 6:6–7

As I grew in the truth of the Scriptures, I began to examine the life-giving ways of Christ in the world around me. Still waiting for my duck call business to take off, I was living off the land to make ends meet. As I worked, I brought my boys and taught them to notice God's creative, life-giving genius. Everything that was created, I told them, was created by him for our good. He created all this for our good, to sustain our life.

On some occasions after the morning chores, the boys and I would sit on the game trails and watch the animals. We'd watch raccoons and foxes. We'd see the occasional snake crossing the path. We'd watch the deer come to feed on the acorns that fell on the trail. I'd pick up one of those acorns and pass it over to Willie or Jason or Al, to feel how small and light it was. I'd point them to the massive oak tree rising over the trail. That tree, I'd tell them, took a couple of hundred years to grow, and it could produce more than twenty tons of timber. It could be felled, sawed into planks, turned into a kitchen table, a full set of chairs, and frame for the house, and there'd still be a good bit of timber left over. All that wood, all of it used to sustain so much life, and it came from a single seed that weighed only an ounce or two.

Wasn't the Almighty creative?

We harvested our fair share of game, mostly ducks and deer, and I taught the boys how the Almighty gave us land to support game, which in turn supported us. He'd given us the best game trails for deer. He'd also blessed us with the perfect feeding ground for the overwintering ducks. We'd call them with our Duck Commander duck calls (also made from wood provided by the Almighty), then we'd take advantage of the perfect shooting lanes. It was almost as if the Almighty had designed all of this just for us, just to sustain our lives through the duck harvest. Life was all around us, I taught them, and God was its Author. It was almost as if he knew what his creation would need to have a full life. It was almost as if he pulled it all together for our support, sustenance, and nourishment.

Those were the days before monetary success, and the life we lived was simple. We didn't have computers or cell phones (I still don't), and I wasn't constantly distracted by business figures, by profits and losses. We weren't distracted by the twenty-four-hour news cycles either. The Robertson family didn't live a decadent life by any stretch of the imagination, but still our life was full. Why? We understood we were not just the product of random chance, of some cluster of cells climbing out of the salt water. No, sir. We knew the truth: Jesus, the Author and Creator of life, filled it all. Knowing that truth, we didn't worry about where our next meal came from or how we'd make ends meet. We trusted the Almighty, and year after year his provision arrangement worked out just fine for us.

Lord, thank you for your wonderful creation that nourishes us. Give me wisdom to share your truth with my children and lead them in your way.

DAY 85 ★ LIVING INTO THE TRUTH

He satisfies the thirsty
  and fills the hungry with good things.
—PSALM 107:9

From the moment I believed, I committed myself to the absolute truth of God's Word. I believed it all, even that he'd provide for me just like the Good Book says. And time after time, he's proved himself faithful to his Word.

Still, living into the truth ain't always easy. It wasn't all roses and daisies as I followed the path the Almighty laid out for me. There were times I wondered how he'd come through, times I thought Miss Kay and I might not make it. In fact, there were two separate occasions when I wondered whether God would keep his promises.

That initial $25,000-dollar loan left us strapped and, as I built Duck Commander, I sold everything but the house, Miss Kay, and the kids so I could make the payments. When the first loan renewal payment came due, Miss Kay and I didn't have the $600 we needed, an amount that wasn't chump change back in those days. Our bank account was down to four digits, including the two numbers after the decimal, and Miss Kay asked whether I'd need to get a job to make ends meet.

I recited the truths of the Bible, said that God would provide for us, his children. I told her we'd trust the Lord's promises. We'd believe all of it or none of it.

The days passed and I kept my eyes peeled. I figured he'd provide. I wondered whether I'd stumble upon a pot of money in the woods or whether I'd come into an inheritance. I didn't know, but I trusted.

On the day the loan was due, I awoke and made my way to the kitchen where Miss Kay was waiting. She asked how we'd make the loan payment, and I shot it to her straight, told her I wasn't sure.

"Let's just wait till the mail runs, and if nothing comes in, I'll march down to the bank and eat my crow," I said.

Secretly, I wondered whether I could find someone to lend me the money. Secretly, I feared the bank would take everything we had.

Around the noon hour, the mail lady pulled up and dropped off the day's mail. In it was a letter from the Bank of Tokyo. It was a certified check for $610, paid in advance for a shipment of calls to Japan. I handed the check to Miss Kay, and she looked at it, looked at me, then looked at the check again before bursting into tears. I told her she could take it to the bank and make the loan payment. She could keep the rest to buy something nice for herself, I said.

I'd relied on the promises of God, knew he'd provide according to his Word of Truth, and I passed the first test.

Lord, forgive me when I focus on my circumstances and not on you. Help me to trust your promise that you will provide for my family.

DAY 86 ★ A RIVER-RAT MIRACLE

Commit your way to the LORD;
   trust in him and he will do this.
—PSALM 37:5

Another $600 loan renewal payment was coming due, so I loaded up my john boat and started fishing the Ouachita. Day after day, net after net, line after line, I came up empty. Every night on my trip back to the house, I prayed and asked God whether he'd come through. And every night I remembered the truth of Scriptures that God would provide for his children.

"Don't worry," I told Miss Kay. "I've staked my life on the truth of God's Word. It says he'll provide for his children. He will."

With a few days to spare before the loan came due, I ran back up the Ouachita and met up with some old farm boys. I explained my predicament and told them I'd need a haul of biblical proportions. They agreed to show me one of their honey holes just upriver. I cruised behind them, but when I looked into the water of their fishing spot, something wasn't right.

"It's too clear," I said. "We need to find some muddier water. Follow me, boys."

They followed me back down to the Louisiana state line. I wasn't as familiar with this stretch, but on our way downriver, I spotted a promising run. There the Ouachita had overflowed the banks and stretched into the woods. There was a yellow, dingy patch of water that'd flooded an old timber road. I pointed to it and told the boys that was the spot.

"Get ready to see a miracle, boys," I said. "The Almighty is with me today. I can feel it."

We began to run the trot line over that flooded timber road, tying one end of the line to a tree, then running it on a diagonal to a tree on the other side. I'd decided to go for broke, decided to tie off a thousand hooks. I'd set them first, then go back and bait them. At least that was the plan. Before I got halfway through tying off the hooks, before I'd baited the first one, the line started jumping. Confused, the boys looked at me.

"Told you. The Almighty is here, boys."

We circled back to the first run and pulled up a hook. Attached to it was one of the largest eel catfish I'd ever caught. We worked the lines back and forth, and they never stopped jumping. Bewildered but amazed, the farm boys jumped in and started helping me take the fish off the line. We worked until the sun had almost set, and before it was over, my boat was almost sunk by the weight of the fish. I gave them a few bucks to help me load up the truck, and we said our goodbyes.

"Mark this date on your calendar, boys. You just witnessed a river-rat miracle."

I drove the catch to market, and lo and behold, it was a miracle. My day's work weighed in at more than one thousand pounds, and the market handed me a note for $780, a note I took to the bank the next day. It allowed us to make the payment and put a little extra in the bank to invest in our young duck call company.

See? When we live in accordance with the Scriptures, when we trust in God, he provides.

★　　★　　★

Lord, may I learn to trust in your provision and give you glory when you meet my needs. Thank you for always providing everything I need and more.

DAY 87 ★ TRAIN UP A CHILD

Start children off on the way they should go,
   and even when they are old they will not turn from it.
—PROVERBS 22:6

As I grew into my role as a father, I wanted to teach my boys about the fruit of a virtuous life. I wanted them to develop good character so they might walk in the blessings of the Almighty. So I did what any other godly river rat with a commercial fishing license might do. I put my boys to work.

When they weren't in school or church, they'd help me run the hoop nets and trotlines, or they'd help me haul fish up from the riverbank. During the summers, they'd help me churn out duck calls on the lathe, a hefty piece of hot-running equipment that was housed in a rusty metal shack. It was hard, sweaty, and low-paying labor, and times being what they were, we didn't have a lot of discretionary money lying around. I was able to give them all they needed, of course, but if they wanted something, they had to work hard and save their money. Industry and frugality, I taught them, went hand in hand.

Day after day they joined me in my labor, and conscious of the little eyes and ears around me, I refrained from cursing or using the name of the Almighty in vain. As we went, I taught them the gospel, how Christ had come to earth, died for our sins, and conquered death. I taught them that a commitment to the life of Christ meant a commitment to keep his words, to pattern our lives after his. We were to be moral, generous, hospitable folks. We were to be Christian.

I taught them to work hard and save their money. I taught them to live moral lives. But I taught them to be kind and respectful to others too. I forbade them from sassing Miss Kay and they wouldn't have considered sassing me. They were also taught to respect their teachers at school and church. They were warned against lashing out in anger and told that if they came to blows, there'd be swift punishment by the man of the house—me.

It wasn't all work and no play, though. I taught them that the Almighty had given us his nature to steward and enjoy. And what could be more enjoyable than duck hunting? Each winter we'd make our way to the blinds, and we'd share a few laughs before harvesting a few birds. We enjoyed each other, and after every hunt I'd remind the boys of my idea of the good life: profitable work, a good wife, a strong family, and a little duck hunting.

Could you ask for anything more?

Lord, thank you for being a kind and patient teacher and guide to me. Help me to be an example to my children and to teach them to work hard, respect authority, and serve you.

DAY 88 ★ A GIFT FOR MARRIAGE

That is why a man leaves his father and mother and is united to his wife, and they become one flesh.
—GENESIS 2:24

There's no mystery about sex and sexuality in the Bible. In the Genesis account we read that God created Adam and Eve—"male and female he created them" (1:27)—and he told them to "be fruitful and increase in number; fill the earth and subdue it" (v. 28). God made us to procreate, to fill the world with humans who'd manage his resources—resources like grain, Arkansas traveler tomatoes, and best of all, ducks. To facilitate this procreation he gave us a gift—sex. That gift was meant to be shared by one man and one woman, and the best I can tell, it was God's original intent that the two would share this gift exclusively within the bonds of their marital union.

It's not just the Genesis account, though, that shows that God's design for sex is within the confines of marriage. Throughout the books of Old Testament law, God shows time and time again how his intent is for sex to be celebrated in marriage. Solomon, one of the wisest men in all of the Scriptures, wrote an entire book about sexuality, showing how it's a gift meant to be shared in marriage, and in the Proverbs he was more explicit about restraining sexual desire, writing:

> May your fountain be blessed,
> and may you rejoice in the wife of your youth.
> A loving doe, a graceful deer . . .
> may you ever be intoxicated with her love.
> Why, my son, be intoxicated with another man's wife?
> Why embrace the bosom of a wayward woman?
>
> (5:18–20)

The New Testament is not silent on the matter either. Throughout the writings to the early church, the apostles gave clear instruction on sex and sexuality. In the earliest days of the church, the truth of Jesus spread to the Gentiles—the hippies, rednecks, and river rats of their day. Among the simplest truths shared with the first church was this: keep your sex in the right place.

Sure, you say, but what exactly does it mean to avoid sexual immorality? How do you keep your sex in the right place? As if to remove all doubt, Paul addressed this issue in his letter to the Corinthian church, writing, "Each man should have sexual relations *with his own wife*, and each woman *with her own husband*. The husband should fulfill his marital duty to his wife, and likewise the wife to her husband" (1 Cor. 7:2–3, emphasis added). To the Hebrews the epistle writer penned a similar instruction: "Marriage should be honored by all, and the marriage bed kept pure, for God will judge the adulterer and all the sexually immoral" (Heb. 13:4).

It doesn't take a brain surgeon to sort out the Scriptures. This ain't rocket science. The instruction of the Scriptures is clear. Sex was made for marriage, for one man and one woman to share within the confines of marriage.

★　　★　　★

Lord, thank you for the gift of sex you designed for husbands and wives. Give me strength to resist the temptations of the world and to stay faithful to the spouse you have given me.

DAY 89 ★ THE REMEDY FOR SEXUAL IMMORALITY

Flee from sexual immorality. All other sins a person commits are outside the body, but whoever sins sexually, sins against their own body.
—1 CORINTHIANS 6:18

Make no mistake; God's Word is true. Sexual immorality comes with a penalty. And if we don't turn back to the truth of God's Word, our society will continue to suffer both here and in the next life. There's a remedy, though. It's a remedy that flows from simple river-rat logic: save your sex for marriage; be disease free; marry a disease-free spouse; keep your sex within the confines of that marriage. The result?

No more unwanted pregnancies. Zero.

No more STDs. Zippo.

No more sexual harassment cases. None. Sounds like a deal.

Of course, I've preached this message for a good many years now, since before I made my first dollar on a duck call. And as I travel and speak more and more, I've protected my commitment to sexual purity by carrying two things with me everywhere I go: my Bible and Miss Kay.

Feasting on the Scriptures and committing to my wife—see? This is what it means to have safe sex. This is what it means to keep your sex safe.

Not everyone appreciates this commitment; that's true enough. It's no secret that I've taken fire over my beliefs. But let me say it straight—I don't hate anyone who's mired in what the Bible calls sin. In fact, I love them. If I truly hated them, I wouldn't share the truth with them. I wouldn't tell them of the saving work of Jesus, to offer them freedom from all their guilt and shame, and to give them an opportunity to live in eternal glory.

So, do I sit in judgment over America's sexual immorality? Nah.

Why should I judge? I haven't lived a sexually perfect life. What's more, it ain't my job to judge. That kind of judgment belongs to the Almighty. And anyway, sitting in judgment is about as useful as cursing the fields for not producing enough millet or smartweed in any given season. Instead of cursing the fields when the food supply runs low, I get to work. And guess what, American Christian? It's time to sow some good spiritual seed, especially as it relates to sexual perversion and immorality. How? I'm glad you asked.

Declare the good and absolute truth of God's Word as it relates to sexuality, even if you've had your own indiscretions. Share the standards of godliness he gave us for our good. Show how a commitment to sexual purity within marriage—one man, one woman, both disease-free—can save folks from heartache, guilt, and shame. Show how it might save our society, too, how it might save us from broken marriages, financial ruin, and so much disease and death. Remind the people in your own communities that a commitment to sexual purity is a commitment to the truth. And don't keep this news from the sexual harassers, perverts, and cheaters. Go to them in love and offer the free gift of Christ to them; offer them deliverance from their sin and shame.

Yes, the truth of the Bible is like millet, and the people of God should sow it everywhere we go in the hopes that the Almighty will turn his favor toward us, that he'll bring us healing and wholeness. Sow it in the hopes that we'll reap the rewards of that harvest. The Word of God—it's the ultimate food supply.

★　★　★

Lord, thank you that you forgive our past sins and give us clear instructions in your Word. Help me to keep my sex safe by feasting on the Scriptures and committing to my spouse.

DAY 90 ★ BUILD YOUR HOME ON A SOLID FOUNDATION

Everyone who hears these words of mine and puts them into practice is like a wise man who built his house on the rock. The rain came down, the streams rose, and the winds blew and beat against that house; yet it did not fall, because it had its foundation on the rock.
—MATTHEW 7:24–25

In 1991, the Robertson homestead was pretty sparse. We were living hand to mouth, still pouring all our money into a business that was just starting to take off. Miss Kay and I were raising our boys in a rickety old home, something that might look like one of today's cheaper modular homes. Our homeplace was thrown together with the materials we had at hand, and to say it wasn't the most structurally sound dwelling might constitute the biggest understatement in this book. Still, we had a roof over our head. We had a sufficient number of beds. There was a furnace. And truth be told, we got along just fine even though we were living well below the poverty line.

Our home had been built on the banks of the river, in the flood-plain. The far end had been built on stilts. During some particularly wet seasons, the water rose all the way to those stilts and settled just below the floorboards. But the water had never risen as high as it did in 1991.

From April through May of that year, our region received something near twenty inches of rain. Day and night, week after week, it was one continuous rainstorm. As it filled the Ouachita basin, worry set in. The water came up, rising up the stilts of our home and settling under the house, less than a foot from the floor. And that's where it stayed for almost a month.

It doesn't take a rocket scientist to understand what happens when warm, stagnant water just sits for a month under a home with exposed plywood flooring. Allow me to share my firsthand experience.

When river water is just a few feet from the underside of your house, the humidity rises and presses up against the underside of that plywood. The plywood wicks up the humidity and holds it in its pores. After a while, moisture-laden plywood loses its structural integrity and becomes something akin to soaked cardboard. And then, even if the water recedes, the floor remains compromised. Even weeks after the water recedes. How do I know?

Early in the morning hours, well before the sun rose over the river, I woke to something that sounded like the house settling just a bit. Then I heard the creaking of shifting flooring. Then something buckled and there was a thunderous cracking sound. Jarred out of bed, I ran into the living room. There, where the couch used to be, was a gaping hole. And as I walked to that hole and looked down, I was greeted by the eyes of Old Blue, my Catahoula Cur, who slept under the house. Neither of us made a sound.

Of course, we replaced the floor. Of course, I used sturdier material the second time around. Of course, we made sure there was a sufficient moisture barrier under the house so we'd never lose another couch and our Catahoula Cur wouldn't be in danger again. But since that night in 1991, the night a kind of sinkhole appeared in my living room, I've come to two conclusions.

First: Don't let your Catahoula sleep under a rotting house.

Second (and more important): If you don't build your house with the right materials, the floor will fall out from under you.

★　　★　　★

Lord, I want to build my life and my family on the solid foundation of your Word. Teach me to live by your Word of Truth so that no matter what comes, we will stand secure in you.

DAY 91 ★ BEFORE THE FIRST BREATH

The word of the LORD came to me, saying,

> "Before I formed you in the womb I knew you,
> before you were born I set you apart;
> I appointed you as a prophet to the nations."

—JEREMIAH 1:4-5

In 1973, the Supreme Court put itself in the seat of the King, deciding what constitutes human life. In *Roe v. Wade*, the Court declared, "The word 'person,' as used in the Fourteenth Amendment, does not include the unborn."[1] A kicking, punching, moving human with a heartbeat, brain activity, and the ability to feel pain was not a person simply because it hadn't been born? Does this make a lick of sense?

Come on now, Your Honors.

I'm no lawyer, and I haven't been trained in the hallowed halls of Harvard or Yale. I've risen to the top of my class here on the river, though, and I've learned a thing or two about the moment when life begins. And really, it's not that hard a concept to grasp, so listen up. Life begins when any living being—tree, flower, egg-encased embryo, or otherwise—takes up space. Consider the following river rat's simple example.

On Day 84 I recalled moments spent with my sons in the woods, how I picked up an acorn of a mighty oak and passed it to one of the boys. I pointed to that tree and described that so much life sprang from that small seed. But how could we know when such a small acorn transformed into something more than just a seed, into something living? Simple. Look at the ground. See the green pushing up out of the hull, rooting down into the Louisiana mud. Was it tiny, particularly when compared to its father oak? Yes. Was it vulnerable to wind, rain, and the hoof of a passing deer? Sure. Still, did that tiny green sprout take up space? No doubt. And would anyone argue the sapling was not alive? Not anyone with a lick of logic. In fact, by my own observations, I suspect the Greenpeacers of the world would agree.

Shouldn't the logic of the tree apply to human life? When a man and a woman come together, when they lie together and bring their unique offerings together in love, something amazing happens. One tiny sperm finds one tiny egg. *Bang!* One tiny embryo forms. The seedling of human life. And in that moment, a new being begins taking up space in the woman's womb.

This rapidly dividing, rapidly growing embryo? Is it life? I suppose if it were an oak tree, there'd be no doubt. And there's no doubt in the mind of the Almighty about human life either. In fact, as far as he's concerned, life begins even *before* conception. He said as much to the prophet Jeremiah:

The word of the LORD came to me, saying,

"Before I formed you in the womb I knew you,
    before you were born I set you apart;
    I appointed you as a prophet to the nations." (1:4–5)

And if Jeremiah would have been conceived these days, if he were an unwanted pregnancy, do you think God would have gone the extra mile to protect his prophet? It's a hypothetical, I know. But I suspect he would have.

From the earliest stages, every embryo has the unique capacity to be a person known by God. Named by God. Called by God to a unique task. Even before the newborn takes its first breath. And King Jesus wants to know and love each human life. The Scriptures share as much.

✶　✶　✶

Lord, thank you for knowing me and choosing me before I took my first breath. Help me to see your image in the life of every precious unborn child you create.

DAY 92 ★ THE VALUE OF LIFE

**Let the little children come to me, and do not hinder them,
for the kingdom of God belongs to such as these.**
—MARK 10:14

To understand the value of life, we need look no further than to the very life of King Jesus himself.

King Jesus, the firstborn of all creation, came into the womb of an unmarried woman (without any need for sex with a man, for what it's worth). He began his life as an embryo, and over nine months he grew in that womb. The King of kings and Lord of lords came to take up space in Mary, and when the time was right, he left that womb and entered the world. From embryo to baby boy. From childhood to adulthood. This was the journey of God with Us. And he made no bones about the worth of the life of a child.

In the Gospels, Jesus makes much of children. Matthew, Mark, and Luke each record a similar story. Parents brought their children to Jesus and asked him to lay hands on them and pray for them. In each story, the disciples (the King's own men) tried to turn the people away, thinking the children were too trivial a matter for Jesus. Seeing their attempts to keep the children from him, Jesus became indignant. Put another way, he was as mad as a hornet. He chastised his disciples and said, "Let the little children come to me, and do not hinder them, for the kingdom of God belongs to such as these" (Mark 10:14; Luke 18:16; Matt. 19:14).

In the gospel of Matthew, the disciples came to Jesus and asked who'd be the greatest in his heavenly kingdom? Was it Peter, the fisher of men? John, the beloved disciple? Maybe it was Mary, his mother. Turning the tables (a thing Jesus was prone to do), he pulled a child into his lap and answered:

Truly I tell you, unless you change and become like little children, you will never enter the kingdom of heaven. Therefore, whoever takes the lowly position of this child is the greatest in the kingdom of heaven. And whoever welcomes one such child in my name welcomes me. (Matt. 18:3–5)

Welcoming a child is like welcoming the King?

If the disciples were slow on the uptake, the religious leaders were even slower. In the days before his execution, as Jesus entered Jerusalem, children gathered in the temple courts and shouted, "Hosanna to the Son of David" (Matt. 21:15). The Scriptures indicate the chief priests and teachers were spitting mad, and they asked, "Do you hear what these children are saying?"

"Yes," Jesus said and then asked, "Have you never read, 'From the lips of children and infants you, Lord, have called forth your praise'?" (v. 16).

See. Even infants praise the King. And if I had my guess, I'd suspect he meant infants in the womb too.

Jesus valued children, the little people of simple faith who always believed, always loved, always praised, and always ran to the King. Their innocence made them the greatest in the kingdom of heaven. And what kind of logic says the greatness of their innocence only begins the day they're born? What kind of logic denies them this dignity while God is forming them in the womb? Do you think King Jesus would snuff out their lives in the womb?

★ ★ ★

King Jesus, thank you for coming to earth as an embryo, to grow in Mary's womb and to show us the value of life. Help me to make much of children and to value the life of every child, as you do.

DAY 93 ★ A FATHER'S DISCIPLINE

[Our human fathers] disciplined us for a little while
as they thought best; but God disciplines us for our
good, in order that we may share in his holiness.
—HEBREWS 12:10

I was raised in a different day and age. A time you might describe as more primitive. We lived in rural Louisiana, and by all measures we were dirt-poor. When we weren't tending the animals, I ran around barefoot with my six brothers and sisters in the yard, the field, the barns, wherever we could find space to play. But all that running around barefoot comes with certain risks. Among them? Roundworm infestation. And so, once a year, my mother dipped into the family savings and called the doctor, who came out to the house to administer a little white pill. A foul-tasting dewormer.

Now I've had a rebellious streak since I came out of the womb. And round about my tenth year, the doc came to administer the dewormer to my siblings and me. We gathered in the living room and stood in a line, hands out and waiting to receive our yearly dose, which we swallowed without water. I hated those pills, so I tossed it over my shoulder and pretended to swallow it. I'd pulled a fast one and gotten away with it. Or so I thought.

Weeks later my mother was cleaning behind the stove, and she swept up that little white pill. She showed us that pill and asked who hadn't taken theirs. I knew it was mine, but if I didn't confess, what could go wrong?

The doctor returned and went down the line, handing out another round of medicine. He watched to make sure each of us put it in our mouths and swallowed it. Mom followed up behind us and issued some medicine of her own. A couple of good old-fashioned swats with

203

a paddle. All seven of us took our pills and a paddling that day, and one by one we were dismissed to the yard.

It wasn't long before my four older siblings pieced together that I was the one responsible for the second dose of medicine and the group swats. And I took a second set of licks, this time from my righteously indignant older siblings. Evidently my siblings ratted me out to my mother, who ratted me out to my father. And when he came home that night, he took a turn at meting out justice. He whupped me for both lying and requiring the doctor to come out for a second call. Doctors weren't cheap, he reminded me. And we didn't have any extra money lying around, he also reminded me.

It wasn't always the easiest way to grow up, especially if you had a rebellious streak. But, still, there was a natural order to the family in those days, an order that kept us in line for the most part. My father and mother were at the top, and they answered only to the Almighty. All the children were subject to parental authority, but the older Robertson kids helped to enforce my parents' rule of law too. And it was this way of being that ensured the survival of the Robertson camp. In fact, it was this rule of law that kept me from getting into too much trouble while I lived under my parents' roof.

Lord, thank you for loving me enough to discipline me. Teach me your ways that I would not sin against you or dishonor your name, and help me to discipline my children with the same compassion and care that you show me.

DAY 94 ★ RAISING A FAMILY GOD'S WAY

Fathers, do not exasperate your children; instead, bring them up in the training and instruction of the Lord.
—EPHESIANS 6:4

When I got out on my own, I denied the family structure my parents hoped to instill in me. I didn't give a lick about the King or the ways he'd instructed his people to operate. I didn't care to be the head of my family or to partner with Miss Kay in bringing up godly children under my roof. Instead, I wanted to party and leave Miss Kay to raise the children. I was more interested in flirting and carousing with any woman who crossed my path. I denied the godly order of family and what did I get for it?

A wife who left me.

Children who didn't know me.

A life that was tearing apart at the seams.

Miss Kay could have divorced me, could have thrown me to the wolves. She didn't, though. Instead, she prayed for me, and when I realized how miserable I was, when I asked her to take me back, she first took me to the preacher, Bill Smith. He helped me to see how broken my life was, how wrecked I was with sin. He shared the good news of King Jesus with me. I followed Christ into the waters of baptism and was introduced to a group of men who taught me what the Bible had to say about becoming a man of God.

I'm happy to say I learned how to be a godly husband to Miss Kay, who took me back. I learned to love, honor, and lead Miss Kay the way the Bible teaches and how to partner with her to raise up our children. I learned how to discipline my children and teach them the good news of the Almighty. I learned the power of embedding our family in the local church.

All these years later, I can attest to the benefits of raising a family the way God intended. Miss Kay and I love each other and like to spend time together. My four boys love the Lord and do their level best to follow him. They're loving husbands and fathers too, and they've trained their kids in the way they should go. What's the result? The Robertson camp is happy, happy, happy.

★　　★　　★

Heavenly Father, thank you for entrusting me with the responsibility to raise children and teach them your ways. Help me to be strong to lead and quick to love, representing you to my family and the world in all I do.

DAY 95 ★ THE CHANGING AMERICAN FAMILY

Children, obey your parents in the Lord, for this is right.
"Honor your father and mother"—which is the first
commandment with a promise—"so that it may go well
with you and that you may enjoy long life on the earth."
—EPHESIANS 6:1-3

The 1960s was an era when professors and politicians declared God was dead and tried to bring about a humanist society. Those were the days of debauchery and hippie living. Those were the days when the American family came under attack. I know. I was there. Although I didn't buy into the humanist philosophy per se, I was all in on the debauchery.

It was a raucous time full of good music and bad thinking. And with the rise of godless teaching in high schools and colleges, with the rise of free love, drugs, and rock and roll, the moral foundations of America began to crack. Our desires led us away from the biblical teachings about sex and the family, and we began empowering politicians who'd give us what we wanted: a shifting of the roles of men and women, freer sex, and easier ways to dissolve our marriages. For the first time in American history, the folks on the Left Coast declared marriage could be terminated by either party for no reason at all.

I'm no social scientist or psychologist, but I know this much: divorce has serious effects on the fabric of our country. It disrupts God's plan, leaving children without a stable mother-father relationship. It destabilizes the loving and instructional environment God intended for children. It often leaves them torn between two parents who can't agree on what's best physically, spiritually, or emotionally for the child. Researchers have noted that children from divorced homes suffer academically, are more likely to be incarcerated for committing a crime as a juvenile, are more likely to live in poverty, and are more likely to engage in underage drinking, drug abuse, and risky sexual behavior.[1]

But do you think these issues only plague the children of divorce in their youth? Is it possible those same problems follow our kids later in life?

Just look around, America.

And if it were only the sky-high rate of divorce that puts the American family in jeopardy, that'd be one thing. But it's not. In 2015, the Supreme Court redefined marriage altogether, claiming that marriage was no longer limited to a relationship between a man and a woman. With its decision that marriage was a fundamental right for same-sex couples, the highest court in the land opened up the floodgates. And now, in this age of easy divorce and same-sex marriage, what constitutes a family? It might be a single mother raising a slew of kids with no father in sight. (And on some occasions this might be warranted.) It might mean a father raising children without a nurturing mother. (And, yes, there might be good reasons for this too.) A family might consist of two men raising a daughter or two women raising a son. The word *family* defies definition and order these days, and we have our godless politicians to thank for this relatively modern experiment.

There is, however, a simple and undeniable truth. Though the American definition of *family* might be in flux, the Word of God is unchanging. The definition of *family* according to King Jesus and his Word trumps any new definition coming out of Washington, DC.

God, you designed the family unit to have order, values, and support. As people all over our nation are struggling with how to define a family, I pray that they will turn back to you and your Word.

DAY 96 ★ GOD'S DESIGN FOR THE FAMILY

Children are a heritage from the LORD,
the fruit of the womb a reward.
—PSALM 127:3 ESV

In the beginning, the Almighty placed Adam in the garden and decided to give him a companion, a helper. Eve. A woman. Adam and Eve kept each other company and brought children into the world. As the Bible records, "That is why a man leaves his father and mother and is united to his wife, and they become one flesh" (Gen. 2:24).

Man and woman were told to be fruitful and multiply, to bear children and populate the earth. And that's exactly what they did and what their children's children did. But having children and raising them isn't just an obligation. It's meant to be a joy. As the psalmist wrote, "Children are a heritage from the LORD, the fruit of the womb a reward" (Psalm 127:3 ESV).

The family—a father and a mother raising children in the way of the Almighty—was the design, and it was meant for the good of society. And knowing us better than we know ourselves, knowing we needed order, the Almighty gave each of us distinct roles in that family unit. What were those roles?

Husbands are to love their wives "as their own bodies. He who loves his wife loves himself. After all, no one ever hated their own body, but they feed and care for their body, just as Christ does the church" (Eph. 5:28–30).

Wives are to "submit yourselves to your own husbands as you do to the Lord. For the husband is the head of the wife as Christ is head of the church, his body, of which he is the Savior" (vv. 22–23). And as an aside, if a husband loves his wife well, this kind of submission shouldn't be burdensome or difficult. Why? Because your husband will consider your opinions, thoughts, gifts, and unique contributions. He'll prize those things above all others.

Parents are placed over the children and tasked with teaching them about the Almighty "when you sit at home and when you walk along the road, when you lie down and when you get up" (Deut. 11:19). Parents are to mete out discipline to their children too. As the Scriptures attest, "Whoever spares the rod hates their children, but the one who loves their children is careful to discipline them" (Prov. 13:24).

And what is the child's place in the order? "Honor your father and your mother, so that you may live long in the land the LORD your God is giving you" (Ex. 20:12). Children are to honor the Almighty by honoring their parents.

There is a natural order to all this, see, and God created that order for our benefit. In that order, husbands love their wives, wives love their husbands, parents love their children, and children love and honor their parents. It's an order that brings stability to a family. In fact, researchers have found that married couples tend to live longer, have better relationships with their children, and their children tend to be healthier.[1]

If we obeyed God's order—one man and one wife loving and submitting to each other and teaching, instructing, and disciplining their children in the Lord—our families would thrive. Just like mine and Miss Kay's. And this shouldn't come as any surprise. After all, the King's ways are much higher than our own.

★　★　★

God, thank you for creating a natural order to the family for our benefit. Help us to obey your order in marriage and parenting so that our family will thrive.

DAY 97 ★ A POLITICAL AWAKENING

Show proper respect to everyone, love the family
of believers, fear God, honor the emperor.
—1 PETER 2:17

On a November morning in 1976, my son Al and I were driving up Highway 165 toward Ouachita Christian High School. Radio on, some DJ in middle Monroe played our favorites: Lynyrd Skynyrd, the Allman Brothers, ZZ Top. And as we pulled into the school parking lot, he interrupted one of our favorites, the Charlie Daniels Band classic "The South's Gonna Do It Again," to announce that Jimmy Carter, the governor from Georgia, had beaten Republican incumbent Gerald R. Ford. Carter would be the next president of the United States.

Truth be told, I wasn't all that politically aware. I knew Uncle Sam had led the troops to war in Vietnam, a war in which our country's armed forces had managed to snatch defeat from the jaws of victory. I knew that in the wake of the war, President Richard Nixon had resigned after authorizing the break-in at the Watergate hotel, the headquarters of the Democratic National Committee. I was vaguely aware that a group of Middle Eastern kings had turned on an oil shortage in 1973 and that oil shortage was driving up gas prices. The country was disenfranchised. I knew that much. And maybe a southern boy from Georgia could turn it around.

"Things are looking up, Al," I said. "The old southerner made it through."

"Maybe so, Dad," Al said.

And that was the extent of our political conversation about the presidential election of 1976. In fact, that'd be the only political conversation I'd have with anyone until 1978.

I was a new Christian in those days, just a year or so removed from my lawless living. I'd been saved by the glorious gospel of our Lord

Jesus Christ, raised from the waters of baptism and into a new life in Jesus. I was living a life of obedience, one committed to prayer, and studying God's Word. I'd been teaching at Ouachita Christian High School and had transformed into a productive member of society. But busy as I was amending my lawless ways, I hadn't spent an ounce of energy on politics.

Politics wasn't a topic we discussed much growing up. In fact, I only recall one political conversation in my childhood. My father had fallen off a drilling rig while on the job in south Louisiana, and he'd busted himself up pretty good. There'd been some discussion about whether he should apply for government assistance, but Dad shot the idea down as soon as it'd taken flight.

"Nah," he said, "we'll manage without the government," and we did.

The community rallied around our dirt-poor family. Church members brought us food. Our neighbors helped us tend to the chores around the house while Dad regained his strength. The months passed, and we managed to make it through none the worse. Dad made it back to the rig, and though he never said it, I received the message loud and clear: river rats needed a government safety net as much as we needed a hole in our hoop nets.

Months passed after the election of 1976, and still I was politically unmotivated. But as I continued to walk into my new life, an odd thing happened. My spiritual epiphany led to a political awakening. And it all started with the Word of God.

★　★　★

God, you are the one who removes kings and establishes kings. As I seek to honor you in my life and my family, give me wisdom to understand how your truth extends to political issues as well.

DAY 98 ★ ALL IN GOD'S FAMILY

Therefore what God has joined together, let no one separate.
—MATTHEW 19:6

King Jesus made his thoughts on the family known. In Matthew 19, the teachers of the law had asked whether divorce was proper. His answer went back to the beginning, back to the Almighty's intention for marriage. He said:

> At the beginning the Creator "made them male and female," and said, "For this reason a man will leave his father and mother and be united to his wife, and the two will become one flesh." . . . Therefore what God has joined together, let no one separate. (vv. 4–6)

The lawmakers asked why Moses allowed the people of Israel to divorce if the Almighty was opposed to it. Jesus answered them, "Moses permitted you to divorce your wives because your hearts were hard. But it was not this way from the beginning" (v. 8).

Jesus didn't just talk about marriage, though. He taught about the role of children too. He taught that children should honor their father and mother, even into adulthood (Matt. 15:4). Jesus taught this kind of honor extended well after the child left the home and extended beyond honoring parents with words but also providing for them materially as they aged (Matt. 15:1–9).

See, from the beginning, the Almighty had a plan in mind, a plan King Jesus affirmed. And it was that plan that would create stable family units and, in turn, a stable society. Those families would give birth to other kingdom-centered families. And through the proliferation of these sorts of King-honoring family units, the love of the King would spread throughout the world. The kingdom would come on earth as it is in heaven.

But what about those who aren't attracted to the opposite sex or would rather not marry and raise children? (Jesus said there'd be eunuchs among us, which I take to mean folks who wouldn't get hitched up with a member of the opposite sex.) Does that mean you have no family responsibilities? No way. Jesus, who was God in the flesh, took no wife himself, but he spoke directly of the kingdom family. The gospel of Mark reported it this way:

> A crowd was sitting around [Jesus], and they told him, "Your mother and brothers are outside looking for you."
>
> "Who are my mother and my brothers?" he asked.
>
> Then he looked at those seated in a circle around him and said, "Here are my mother and my brothers! Whoever does God's will is my brother and sister and mother." (3:31–35)

Paul, a devout follower of King Jesus who gave us the majority of the New Testament, was unmarried, and he devoted his singleness to the glory of God. He worked tirelessly to spread the gospel of Christ, and he encouraged others to stay unmarried so long as they could control their desires (1 Cor. 7:8–9).

Followers of the Almighty, we're all in the family and we all have familial duties. We're all responsible to support the family structure ordained by God, all responsible to teach and train the children, all responsible to come together in a larger family that worships the King. And with that comes a certain kind of responsibility, namely, the responsibility to speak up for the Almighty's family structure in every facet of our lives, including in the political arena.

★　　★　　★

Heavenly Father, thank you that I am part of your family. May I be faithful to fulfill my familial duties by supporting a biblical family structure, teaching children to know and love you, and meeting together in a church family that worships you.

DAY 99 ★ THE KIND OF FAMILY GOD HONORS

Trust in the LORD with all your heart
and lean not on your own understanding;
in all your ways submit to him,
and he will make your paths straight.
—**PROVERBS 3:5-6**

In 2012, *Duck Dynasty*—a show about our God-fearing, gun-toting, redneck family—swept Middle America. We owned our time slot and had millions of viewers. Over eleven seasons, we drew viewers from across the country, particularly from the South and the Midwest, that so-called flyover portion of the country that so many politicians talk about these days. We were unconventional for a television family. We didn't cuss or drink. We prayed on television. We spoke about God openly. We loved each other and lived out God's intention for family as best we could. And as we did, our popularity only rose.

I can't exactly say why *Duck Dynasty* was so popular, but I have an educated guess. I reckon the American people were waiting to see a functional family they could identify with, maybe even aspire to. They wanted to see men who were godly men, who worked hard, played hard, taught the gospel in every facet of their lives, and weren't mocked at every turn by their wives. They wanted to see godly women who honored God, cared for their family and community, and were loved by their husbands. It gave them hope to see children respecting their parents (at least for the most part) and living lives of intentional faith. The American people needed to believe the God-centered family was still important to American life.

We've done our best to create the kind of family the Almighty honors. One man, loving one wife, raising children to love, honor, and serve the King. It's an atypical family structure in America these days, one the politicians (which is to say nothing about Hollywood) seem determined to destroy. Still, we've reaped the benefits of it, such as peace, prosperity, and a family in which every member knows they're loved.

The godless politics of men can't change the family structure set forth by the Almighty, no matter how hard they try. But if they keep undermining God's design, America will continue to suffer the consequences as a country. What consequences?

A lack of discipline.

Increased violence.

Increased rates of depression.

A country of godless, senseless, loveless, self-absorbed, self-indulgent, uncommitted people.

Sound like the kind of country you want to live in? Not me. So as you're considering which political candidates to vote for and which policies to support, ask yourself whether they're aligned with the family values of the King.

And if there's no perfect candidate (there never is these days), ask yourself, *At the very minimum, who won't get in the way of applying Jesus Politics as it relates to the family?* Then, march into the public square and declare the Almighty's truth about the family. Support organizations that advocate traditional, biblical views of marriage. Finally, walk into the voter booth and prayerfully cast your vote in a way that aligns with the King, blesses the citizens of the kingdom, and promotes the King's family design for all humankind. Then rest knowing that when you protect the American family, you're protecting America herself.

★ ★ ★

Lord, I commit to raise my family according to your Word. Please guide me to make my family one that will bring honor to you and be an example of intentional faith to others.

DAY 100 ★ SHARE YOUR FAITH, DO GOOD, AND CHANGE LIVES

Preach the word; be prepared in season and
out of season; correct, rebuke and encourage—
with great patience and careful instruction.
—2 TIMOTHY 4:2

We were in New York City, doing an interview with *Varney & Co.* I opened the interview by sharing how all have fallen short of the glory of God, all are living under the law of sin, and all would die. I shared how every human needed the saving work of Jesus and how it was my hope to share that truth with as many people as I could.

At the end of the interview, I closed with a message that might change America if we'd let it. "Love God, love each other. It's the message of the Bible," I said.

I shared the truth with Mr. Varney just like I had with so many, whether paupers or presidents. I was clear. Unashamed. And interview after interview that day, I continued to do the same thing.

After a couple of days of publicity appearances, we made our way back to Northern Louisiana. There, I got back to my morning routine: setting out the crawfish traps, tending to the fields, sitting in the woods and watching the morning roll by. As I did, I considered that weeklong trip, how it'd been a success as far as I was concerned. We'd gone to New York for one reason: to share the good news of Jesus and to invite people to turn to the Almighty and live good and godly lives. We shared how if enough people lived these kinds of good and godly kingdom lives, they might change America if we'd let it. And as far as I could tell, millions had heard that message.

I do my best to carry my faith everywhere I go. As far as I can tell, so do my boys and their families. The Robertson camp lives their faith out loud in the public sector. We preach it on television shows,

217

podcasts, and in books. But we don't just share it when the cameras are rolling. We live it out in our day-to-day lives too.

- We read the Word of God every day and attend Bible studies because we're followers of the King.
- We pray with family and friends because we're followers of the King.
- We share our faith with anyone who crosses our path because we're followers of the King.
- We get up early, work hard, and don't complain because we're followers of the King.
- We honor our parents, our wives, and our neighbors because we're followers of the King.
- We help women who're on their way to the abortion clinics because we're followers of the King.
- We share our bounty, our catfish, our crawfish, and our money with our neighbors because we're followers of the King.
- We speak to those in our community about godless socialism, religious liberty, marriage, and the family because we're followers of the King.
- We have conversations with politicians and media personalities that never make the news. Why? You guessed it. Because we're followers of the one and only eternal King.

We're out to change America one life at a time. How do we do that? We share the love of Jesus in word *and* in deed. We "strive to do what is good for each other and for everyone else" (1 Thess. 5:15). And what does it mean to do good? It means doing just as Jesus would. And this is what I call *kingdom living*.

★   ★   ★

King Jesus, help me to carry my faith in you wherever I go. Give me the courage and opportunity to share the good news and invite people to turn to the Almighty and live good and godly kingdom lives.

NOTES

Day 1: Is God Dead?

1. John T. Elson, "Toward a Hidden God," Time, April 8, 1966, https://time
   .com/vault/issue/1966-04-08/page/98/.
2. Frank Newport, "Most Americans Still Believe in God," *Gallup*, June 29,
   2016, https://news.gallup.com/poll/193271/americans-believe-god,aspx.

Day 15: Speaking the Truth in Love

1. Drew Magary, "What the Duck?" *GQ*, December 17, 2013, https://www
   .gq.com/story/duck-dynasty-phil-robertson?currentPage=2.
2. Drew Magary, "What the Duck?"

Day 27: The Value of Virtue

1. Independence Hall Association, "In His Own Words," *The Autobiography
   of Benjamin Franklin*, http://www.ushistory.org/franklin/autobiography
   /page38.htm.
2. "In His Own Words," *The Autobiography of Benjamin Franklin*.
3. George Washington, "Farewell Address," September 19, 1796, The Papers
   of George Washington, University of Virginia, Charlottesville, http://
   gwpapers.virginia.edu/documents_gw/farewell/transcript.html.
4. George Washington, "General Orders, 2 May 1778," National Archives
   Founders Online, https://founders.archives.gov/documents/Washington
   /03-15-02-0016.
5. "From John Adams to Thomas Jefferson, 19 April 1817," Founders
   Online, National Archives, https://founders.archives.gov/documents
   /Adams/99-02-02-6744.
6. "John Adams Diary 1, 18 November 1755–29 August 1756," February
   22, 1756, *Adams Family Papers: An Electronic Archive,* Massachusetts
   Historical Society, https://www.masshist.org/digitaladams/archive/.

Day 32: Individual Liberties

1. Thomas Jefferson, "Notes on the State of Virginia, Query XVIII:
   Manners," Teaching American History, http://teachingamericanhistory.
   org/library/document/notes-on-the-state-of-virginia-query-xviii-manners/.
2. Benjamin Franklin, "Silence Dogood, No. 8," printed in *New-England*

Courant, July 9, 1722, National Archives Founders Online, https:// founders.archives.gov/documents/Franklin/01-01-02-0015.

Day 35: Religious Liberty

1. Caleb Parke, "Ohio School Scrubs 92-Year-Old Ten Commandments Plaque After Atheists Complain," Fox News, July 1, 2019, https://www .foxnews.com/us/ohio-school-atheist-complain-ten-commandments.
2. David G. Savage, "Colorado Cake Maker Asks Supreme Court to Provide a Religious Liberty Right to Refuse Gay Couple," *Los Angeles Times*, September 12, 2017, https://www.latimes.com/politics/la-na-pol-court -religion-gays-20170912-story.html.

Day 36: The Freedom to Bear Arms

1. U.S. Constitution Amendment II, America's Founding Documents, The Bill of Rights: A Transcription, National Archives, https://www.archives .gov/founding-docs/bill-of-rights-transcript#toc-amendment-ii-2.
2. George Washington to Alexander Hamilton, May 2, 1783, Mount Vernon, The Washington Library Center for Digital History, https:// www.mountvernon.org/library/digitalhistory/quotes/article/it-may-be-laid -down-as-a-primary-position-and-the-basis-of-our-system-that-every -citizen-who-enjoys-the-protection-of-a-free-government-owes-not-only-a -proportion-of-his-property-but-even-his-personal-services-to-the -defence-of-it-and-consequently-that-th/.
3. Thomas Jefferson to William Stephens Smith, November 13, 1787, Library of Congress, Washington, DC, https://www.loc.gov/exhibits /jefferson/105.html.

Day 39: A Kingdom Foundation

1. Noah Webster to James Madison, October 16, 1829, Founders Early Access, Rotunda, University Press of Virginia, Charlottesville, https:// rotunda.upress.virginia.edu/founders/default.xqy?keys=FOEA-print-02 −02–02–1897.
2. George Washington, "Farewell Address," September 19, 1796, The Papers of George Washington, University of Virginia, Charlottesville, http:// gwpapers.virginia.edu/documents_gw/farewell/transcript.html.
3. George Washington, "General Orders, 2 May 1778," National Archives

Founders Online, https://founders.archives.gov/documents/Washington/03-15-02-0016.

Day 40: The Kingdom That Endures

1. John Adams to Thomas Jefferson, June 28, 1813, quoted by Michael Novak, "Meacham Nods," *National Review,* December 13, 2007, https://www.nationalreview.com/2007/12/meacham-nods-michael-novak/.
2. See "John Adams Diary 1, 18 November 1755–29 August 1756," February 22, 1756, *Adams Family Papers: An Electronic Archive,* Massachusetts Historical Society, Boston, https://www.masshist.org/digitaladams/archive/.
3. George Morgan, *The True Patrick Henry* (Philadelphia: Lippincott, 1907), 415.

Day 46: Healing the Gun-Violence Crisis

1. John Gramlich and Katherine Schaeffer, "7 Facts About Guns in the U.S.," FactTank, Pew Research Center, October 22, 2019, https://www.pewresearch.org/fact-tank/2019/10/22/facts-about-guns-in-united-states/.

Day 76: God's Precise Creation

1. For a helpful diagram illustrating how the earth's tilt affects the seasons, see "Resource Library: Encyclopedia Entry: Axis," National Geographic, accessed November 29, 2019, https://www.nationalgeographic.org/encyclopedia/axis/.

Day 91: Before the First Breath

1. Roe v. Wade, 410 U.S. at 158 (1973).

Day 95: The Changing American Family

1. Amy Desai shares this research in her *Focus on the Family* article, "How Could Divorce Affect My Kids?" January 1, 2007, https://www.focusonthefamily.com/marriage/how-could-divorce-affect-my-kids/.

Day 96: God's Design for the Family

1. Bradford Wilcox, *Why Marriage Matters: Twenty-six Conclusions from the Social Sciences,* 2nd ed. (New York: Institute for American Values, 2005), http://americanvalues.org/catalog/pdfs/why_marriage_matters2.pdf.

ABOUT THE AUTHOR

Phil Robertson is a professional hunter who invented his own duck call and founded the successful Duck Commander Company. He also starred in the popular television series on A&E, *Duck Dynasty*, and is now the host of the new subscription television series *In the Woods with Phil* on BlazeTV.com. He is a *New York Times* bestselling author of *Jesus Politics; The Theft of America's Soul; Happy, Happy, Happy;* and *UnPHILtered*. He and his wife, Kay, live in West Monroe, Louisiana. He has five children, eighteen grandchildren, and seven great-grandchildren.